T0323868

STATISTICAL ANALYSIS

Statistical Analysis: The Basics provides an engaging and easy-to-read primer on this sometimes daunting subject. Intended for those with little or no background in mathematics or statistics, this book explores the importance of statistical analysis in the modern world by asking statistical questions about data and explains how to conduct such analyses and correctly interpret the results.

Packed with everyday examples from sport, health, education, and leisure, it reinforces the understanding of core topics while avoiding the heavy use of equations and formulae. Written in a highly accessible style and adopting a hands-on approach, each chapter is accompanied by a summary of key points, illustrations and tables, and recommendations for further reading, with the final chapter delving into the practicalities of conducting a real-life statistical research project.

Statistical Analysis: The Basics is essential reading for anyone who wishes to master the fundamentals of modern-day statistical analysis.

Christer Thrane is a Sociologist and a Professor at Inland Norway University of Applied Sciences.

The Basics Series

The Basics is a highly successful series of accessible guidebooks which provide an overview of the fundamental principles of a subject area in a jargon-free and undaunting format.

Intended for students approaching a subject for the first time, the books both introduce the essentials of a subject and provide an ideal springboard for further study. With over 50 titles spanning subjects from artificial intelligence (AI) to women's studies, *The Basics* are an ideal starting point for students seeking to understand a subject area.

Each text comes with recommendations for further study and gradually introduces the complexities and nuances within a subject.

COUPLE THERAPY
MOLLY LUDLAM

BDSM and Kink
STEFANI GOERLICH AND ELYSSA HELFER

Simone de Beauvoir
MEGAN BURKE

Interviewing: The Basics
MARK HOLTON

Shakespeare (fourth edition)
SEAN MCEVOY

DREAMS
DALE MATHERS AND CAROLA MATHERS

JEWISH ETHICS
GEOFFREY D. CLAUSSEN

MODERN ARCHITECTURE
GRAHAM LIVESEY

MICROECONOMICS
THOMAS R. SADLER

STATISTICAL ANALYSIS
CHRISTER THRANE

For a full list of titles in this series, please visit www.routledge.com/The-Basics/book-series/B

STATISTICAL ANALYSIS

THE BASICS

Christer Thrane

Routledge
Taylor & Francis Group

LONDON AND NEW YORK

Designed cover image: DrAfter123 / Getty Images ®

First published 2025
by Routledge
4 Park Square, Milton Park, Abingdon, Oxon OX14 4RN

and by Routledge
605 Third Avenue, New York, NY 10158

Routledge is an imprint of the Taylor & Francis Group, an informa business

British Library Cataloguing-in-Publication Data
A catalogue record for this book is available from the British Library

Library of Congress Cataloging-in-Publication Data
Names: Thrane, Christer, author.
Title: Statistical analysis: the basics / Christer Thrane.
Description: Abingdon, Oxon; New York, NY: Routledge, 2025. |
Series: The basics | Includes bibliographical references and index.
Identifiers: LCCN 2024036952 | ISBN 9781032640785 (hardback) |
ISBN 9781032640778 (paperback) | ISBN 9781032640808 (ebook)
Subjects: LCSH: Social sciences—Research—Statistical methods. |
Research—Statistical methods.
Classification: LCC HA29 .T549 2025 | DDC 519.5–dc23/eng/20220224
LC record available at https://lccn.loc.gov/2024036952

ISBN: 978-1-032-64078-5 (hbk)
ISBN: 978-1-032-64077-8 (pbk)
ISBN: 978-1-032-64080-8 (ebk)

DOI: 10.4324/9781032640808

Typeset in Bembo
by codeMantra

CONTENTS

FIGURES

TABLES

FOREWORD AND ACKNOWLEDGMENTS

Over the past seven years, I have written a series of textbooks exploring various facets of statistical analysis. Two of these – Thrane (2020) on regression analysis and Thrane (2022) on quantitative research methods – were published by Routledge. In addition, four similar books in Norwegian were published by Cappelen Damm Akademisk and Humanist Forlag. In the interest of transparency, I have incorporated some of the material I found most illuminating in my previous books into this one, albeit with some tweaking and tinkering. I also began sharing my thoughts on statistics through blog posts on Medium.com late in 2023, and some of those posts have been adapted for inclusion in this book.

Thanks to Michelle Gallagher for the opportunity to publish this book as a part of Routledge's "Basics Series." A big thank you also goes out to the anonymous reviewers who helped organize my thoughts for the book at the outset. Thanks again to everyone providing me with helpful feedback on my earlier books. Finally, thanks to Nicholas Myers for constructive comments on a first and almost complete draft of this book. All remaining mistakes and ambiguities are solely my responsibility.

Blogs on statistics on Medium.com:
https://medium.com/@christerthrane
ResearchGate:
https://www.researchgate.net/profile/Christer-Thrane
GitHub:
https://github.com/christer-thrane
Web page:
https://www.inn.no/english/find-an-employee/christer-thrane.html

PREFACE
What the book is about and what it is not about

What the book is about

Results of statistical analysis are omnipresent, constantly surrounding us. To obtain such results, someone has put a statistics program to analyze a bunch of numbers we in our modern-day era call data. Statistical analyses and results are often driven by policy-relevant questions for business and governance. Yet they might also be the output of a researcher testing a hypothesis or the yield of a layperson's curiosity. And sometimes, and perhaps more often than many find reassuring, statistical results seem to be produced for no discernible reason whatsoever.

Many people have for valid reasons formed the opinion that turning data into statistical results – that is, doing statistical analysis – is a difficult, boring, or immaterial process. I beg to differ, and this book is my response to that claim. Here, I hope to show that doing statistical analysis can be interesting and worthwhile. Sometimes it is also exciting in the sense that learning something new can border on fun or at least be stimulating. Also, and again as I hope to show you rather than tell you, statistical analysis is typically not technically difficult if you are willing to trust your statistics program's calculating abilities. You should!

In essence, this book takes on asking statistical questions about data, analyzing data, interpreting the results of data analyses, and presenting these results. But this should be mentioned at the start: much can go wrong in the process from data collection to the final interpretation and presentation of statistical results. We'll explore these potential pitfalls in Chapter 7. First, though, we must learn to use the tools to do so in Chapters 2–6. Chapter 8 brings the book to a close. This final chapter has a typical hands-on approach, delving into the practicalities of conducting a real-life statistical research project.

What the book is not about

The science of statistics contains the bag of tricks used for statistical analysis. That said, this is not a book on statistics. Rather, I pick and choose in a case-by-case manner what I need from the statistical mothership to do, interpret, and present the statistical analysis in question. Neither is this a book about a specific statistics program, although I'll show you two outputs (!) from such programs. Still, all the results in the book should be straightforward to reproduce in statistics programs like Stata, R, or SPSS. The data used in the book is accessible on the book's website.

INTRODUCTION

Statistical analysis as an investigative tool

DOI: 10.4324/9781032640808-1

STATISTICS: DO WE REALLY HAVE TO?

I won't beat around the bush. Statistics often gets a bad rep, and the culprit is statistics itself. More precisely, the reason many find statistics difficult, boring, or irrelevant has to do with how it has been taught during the last 50 years or so. I see no need to dwell on the negative in what I hope will be an upbeat book. But we must concede that the teaching methods, textbooks, and school exams have created the widespread misconception that statistical analysis is all about memorizing formulas, doing calculations by hand, and solving irrelevant algebraic equations. Therefore, let me start off by busting two persistent myths:

(1) Practical statistical analysis is *not* about memorizing formulas, doing arithmetic calculations, and solving algebraic equations.
(2) Practical statistical analysis is *not* difficult in the technical sense.

Contrary to popular belief, and as I aim to show in this book, statistical analysis is about finding out things. We use statistical analysis to become more knowledgeable in some respect. In essence, thus, statistical analysis is an *investigative* tool. The investigative mode of thought sparking a statistical analysis may be the result of curiosity, as in seeking new knowledge for fun or its own sake. Or it could have a more practical (research) justification, like solving a current problem or reducing future uncertainties. Regardless, what should drive a statistical analysis is an inquisitive mindset with the goal of uncovering something new. Sure, we know a lot but there is always more to learn.

No one in the history of statistics embodies this spirit of inquisitiveness better than Sir Francis Galton (1822–1911). Galton had a curiosity about all sorts of things and a knack for measuring them: from fingerprints and sweet peas to people's stature.[1] Thanks to his inquisitive mind, his love for measurement, and his habit of systematically recording his findings, Galton is arguably the godfather of modern-day statistical analysis. To set the stage for this book, let's look at some of his discoveries through the lens of statistical analysis. As we shall see later, especially in Chapters 3, 5, 6, and 8, Galton's thinking and insights paved the way for the typical method of associating one phenomenon with another in modern thought and statistical research settings.

FRANCIS GALTON AND HUMAN HEREDITY

Much inspired by his half-cousin Charles Darwin (1809–1882), Galton was intrigued by how physical traits seemed to be passed down from parents and grandparents to the next generation in both humans and animals. Keeping this in mind, he measured the stature of 481 adult sons as well as the stature of their fathers. Furthermore, he wrote down all his measurements as in Table 1.1. I show the numbers for only five (fictitious) sons out of the 481 to save us some page space. (Obviously!)

Galton was all about figuring out how traits were passed down from one generation to the next. To get a better picture of this, he constructed what we today call a scatterplot of the sons' and their fathers' statures based on the information in Table 1.1. And he did this all by hand and by eye, no fancy computers! Our modern-day version of this plot is shown in Figure 1.1.

Each dot in the plot shows a son's height paired with his father's height in inches, and the shape it makes is pretty telling. Most of the sons are located either in the lower left or in the upper right quadrant of the plot. In this way, the plot shows a clear, systematic pattern: sons of taller fathers tend to be taller themselves, and sons of shorter fathers tend to be shorter themselves. This trend is even more obvious in Figure 1.2, where I have added a straight line that sums up the general relationship between the sons' and their fathers' heights.

By plotting the sons' and their fathers' height on a vertical y-axis and a horizontal x-axis (aka a coordinate system), Galton managed by way of statistical reasoning to show how a genetic trait like stature gets passed down from one generation to the next. And he

Table 1.1 Galton's measurements of stature for five adult sons and their fathers

Son's name	Son's height in inches	Father's height in inches
Andrew (1)	68	67
Geoff (2)	73	72
Michael (3)	72	71
Anthony (4)	76	77
...	...	...
...	...	...
George (481)	67	66

Note. 70 inches (or 5 feet 10 inches) is roughly 178 centimeters.

did this just through statistical reasoning – no formulas, no manual calculations, and no algebraic equations needed. Neither Figure 1.1 nor Figure 1.2 is difficult to grasp in the technical sense. In fact, their main message practically jumps out at you.

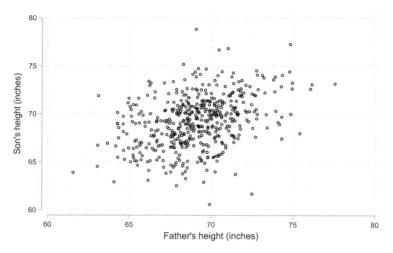

Figure 1.1 Scatterplot of Galton's data

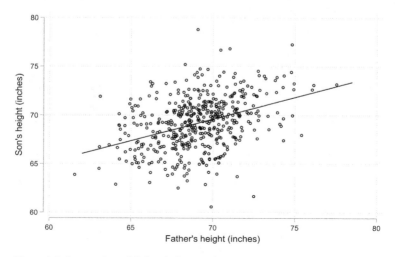

Figure 1.2 Scatterplot of Galton's data, with general trend line superimposed

DATA, UNITS, AND VARIABLES

Galton invented the idea of associational statistical analysis in no small amount as a by-product of his thirst for knowledge about human heredity. Yet since many of the key concepts we still use in today's statistical analysis were already (implicitly) present in Galton's endeavors, I briefly mention these below. I have much more to say on these matters in Chapters 2 and 3.

So, if statistical analysis is an inquisitive tool, what do we exactly investigate? The answer is a bunch of numbers arranged in columns and rows. Formally, we call this collection of numbers our *data* or our *data set*. (Some prefer data frame; I do not.) Although the term "data" was not thought up in Galton's days (by the way, data are plural), we would in modern-day speak call his measurements of sons' and fathers' stature for Galton's data or data set. Note the typical row/column-structure in Table 1.1, which also is called a data-matrix.

The units in Galton's data were 481 adult sons.[2] Typically, we gather data on someone or something, and we call these entities our units or observations. I use the term "units" in this book. People are the units in many statistical analyses in the social and behavioral sciences. But units might also be something made by people: cars, houses, stocks, wars, bottles of beer, stays in hotels, accidents, you name it. Other (aggregate) units are schools, firms, municipalities, and countries. The units typically make up the rows in a data set, with one row for each unit. So, in Galton's data, one son occupies his own row.

We talk about phenomena and things in everyday life. In statistics, we call these variables. Variables are the phenomena or things we measure for our units; we have variable information on our units. In Galton's data, the two variables were the sons' height and their fathers' height. In general, a variable is something that varies between or among units. So, some of the sons (units) in Galton's data were short, some were tall, and a whole bunch were somewhere in the middle. The same was evident for their fathers. Variables most often make up the columns in a data set, with one column for each variable. And to keep things organized, a variable's name often sits right at the top of its column.

Some variables we like to think of as being dependent, while others are independent. Distinguishing between these is crucial when we want to associate one variable to another variable, as Galton did. The dependent variable is *dependent* on the independent variable. Galton's case is instructive. Sons' height (the dependent variable) is dependent on fathers' height (the independent variable). A son's height cannot determine his father's height; it must be the other way around. Telling apart the dependent and independent variable is easy in Galton's case. In other cases, however, distinguishing between dependent and independent variables is not always so clear-cut. I return to this in Chapter 3. But for now, let's get back to the present.

BACK TO PRESENT-DAY STATISTICAL ANALYSIS

Suppose 12,000 patients stayed for one or more nights in Hospital A during 2023. Your detective mission is to figure out how many nights a typical patient stayed. Now, imagine getting access to data showing the number of nights each patient stayed in the hospital. Such data would look a bit like the ones you see in Table 1.2, where I for reasons of page space show the results for only the first four patients and the last one. Note the similarity in structure to Galton's data in Table 1.1. The patients are the units, and the number of nights a patient stayed is the only variable. Some patients stayed for more nights than others, as to be expected.

Assume for a second that the numbers in Table 1.2 were all your data. How would you go about finding out how many nights a typical patient stayed? One approach would be to add the individual stays (the number of nights stayed by each patient) and divide the sum you get

Table 1.2 Data on number of nights spent at Hospital A for five patients (out of 12,000)

Patient number	Number of nights stayed in hospital A
Patient 1	2
Patient 2	5
Patient 3	1
Patient 4	4
...	...
...	...
Patient 12,000	3

by five (the number of patients in total): $(2 + 5 + 1 + 4 + 3)/5 = 3$. The *average* stay is three nights. Not terribly difficult that one.

A second approach first involves arranging the stays in ascending order: 1, 2, 3, 4, and 5. The number in the middle of this ascending distribution of stays is the *median*: 3. Both the average and the median answer the question of how many nights a typical patient stayed. Precisely, the average is the typical number of nights stayed in the data, whereas the median is the number of nights stayed by the typical patient in the data. Not terribly difficult this one either, although a bit more subtle.

But your job is not to find out how many nights a typical patient stayed for based on the data in Table 1.2. Your objective is to get this information for a larger pool of 12,000 patients. Obviously, the task of calculating this number by hand is a non-starter. Thankfully, we have statistics programs designed to handle such computations in a fraction of a second. This brings us back to an essential point made earlier: to unravel the hidden information we are curious about in our data, like the average or the median, we use a statistics program to do our arithmetic calculations.

VARIABLES' MEASUREMENT LEVEL

Variables are a mixed bag; they come in all sorts of forms. One basic way to categorize them is into quantitative and categorical variables. Quantitative variables have values that are actual numbers, like the height in inches in Galton's data or the number of nights stayed in our hospital data.[3] Since these numbers can be sorted in ascending or descending order, and since the distance from one to four is the same as the distance from six to nine, we can compare the units in terms of their score on the variable in question. Also, averages and medians make perfect sense for such variables. On the flip side, and as the name implies, categorical variables are this-or-that variables. Your birth country can be England, France, Belgium, Australia, the USA, etc., but it can only be one. Similarly, people are typically born as either male or female biologically. But you cannot really compare or rank birth country or biological sex in terms of being higher or lower (or more or less). To give a sneak peek of Chapter 2, the takeaway here is that a variable's *measurement level* puts restrictions on what kind of statistical questions it makes sense to ask.

STATISTICS AND STATISTICAL ANALYSIS: THE KEY IDEA

Statistics are everywhere; its findings seep into every corner of our modern-day life. Be it behavioral or social research, medical research, insurance, manufacturing, engineering, astronomy, agriculture, accounting, education, sports, betting, or even card games – you name it, statistics is there. Usually, we use statistical analysis to get answers for data on a heap of units – like our 12,000 patients above. The goal is to dig out the hidden knowledge tucked away in the data, and the pickaxe for this job is statistical reasoning; we use statistical analyses to unearth what lies below the surface. Finding the average number of nights stayed among 12,000 patients is thus a process of simplification to find the typical length of stay. Not too long ago, this simplification of finding the average or median – a kind of aggregation process – was considered revolutionary. Somewhat paradoxical, we gain knowledge about all our units (in this case: patients) by throwing away information on our individual units, as elegantly put by Stigler (2016, p. 4).

We do statistical analysis to simplify what the complex data are hiding. Without this simplification, our brains would not be capable of comprehending what the data patterns look like. It is thus ironic that many people for good reasons find statistics anything but simple. The main culprit, as I hinted at in the introduction, is Statistical Science itself. It has mostly failed in communicating this key insight. So, my not-so-moderate aim in this book is to show you, and not only to tell you, how to think statistically when you want to gain knowledge about something that, at least for now, is hidden in your data.

SMALL DATA, BIG DATA, MACHINE LEARNING, AND ARTIFICIAL INTELLIGENCE (AI)

When Galton collected his data (in our present-day speak, that is) about the adult sons' stature at the end of the 19th century, his data would have been considered big. Today, however, we would label them borderline small. What changed? Well, in its most basic sense, "big data" means data with thousands of rows (units) and hundreds or more columns (variables). Big literally means bigger. But with the advent of fast computers, the vertical size of a data set (the number of units) soon became less of an issue for statistical analysis. For instance, calculating the average length of a hospital stay among 12,000 patients might have taken about 14 seconds on a personal computer in 1987, whereas the same procedure among 120,000 patients took perhaps 0.30 seconds in 2023.

In a more dynamic sense, "big data" refers to data that are massive (many units/variables), complex (does not fit into one data matrix), and continuous (continuously collected, stored, and updated).[4] Think of data from websites, search logs, mobile phones, cameras, sensors, wearable devices – you get the picture. With big data often boasting hundreds or thousands of variables (columns), one of the challenges in statistical analysis is figuring out which should be the dependent and independent variables. (Galton had not so much to choose from.) This is where data mining and machine learning techniques, powered by AI, come into play. Such techniques are getting increasingly popular for picking out the most "appropriate" variables. I'm not going to analyze big data in this book, though. My stance here is that you should understand how to analyze small data before scaling up to big data. And then this will be no big deal.

CURIOSITY DID NOT KILL THE CAT: THE BOOK'S STRUCTURE AND PEDAGOGICAL APPROACH

The premise of this book should now hopefully be crystal clear. Fueled by curiosity and an inquisitive mind, we do statistical analysis to learn something new about our data. The questions we aim to answer tend to fall into one of three categories: descriptive questions, associational questions, and inferential questions. And since the answers we get from descriptive questions have consequences for the associational and inferential questions, we typically tackle these questions in that order. This also sets the stage for the upcoming chapters: we'll start with descriptive questions (Chapter 2), then move on to associational questions (Chapter 3), before taking on inferential questions (Chapter 4).

Let's provide a quick sneak peek of what is to come in this book:

Chapter 2 is all about describing phenomena, which we now know as variables in a data set. These descriptions usually revolve around finding out what is typical for a variable. Here are a few example questions, some of which will be answered in later chapters:

-   How many goals does a player in a top-tier football league typically score in a season?

- How much does one typically have to pay for a beer?
- How much money does a tourist typically spend on a vacation trip?
- What is the typical number of doctor visits for an employee in a year?
- What is the typical score in a school exam?
- What is the typical number of reported crimes in a month for London?
- How much is the typical total bill for a restaurant meal?
- What is the typical income of a top-notch athlete?

These what–is–typical questions also have a lot to do with statistical variation (or dispersion) and with how this variation is distributed. Chapter 2 will also look at this in more detail, so stay tuned!

Chapter 3 dives into how variables are associated with or relate to other variables, much in the spirit of Galton's pioneering work.[5] Galton discovered that adult sons' height was associated with their fathers' height, and such variable associations are the cornerstone of much present-day statistical research. For example:

- Is the number of goals scored in a football season associated with players' age or position on the pitch? If so, how?
- Is the price of a beer associated with its alcohol content or its production country? If so, how exactly?
- Is tourism spending associated with length of stay or type of destination? With tourists' age? If so, how does that work?
- Is the number of doctor visits among employees associated with their age or their education level? If so, in what way?
- Is an exam score associated with hours of preparation or the numbers of missed lectures? If so, how?
- Is the number of reported crimes in London each month associated with the amount of rainfall per month or the temperature? If so, in what way?
- Is the total bill for a restaurant meal associated with the number of diners or dishes being served? If so, how exactly?
- Is the income of top–notch athletes associated with their recent performances or age? If so, in what way?
- Is the test-score in a medical trial associated with whether patients got to eat actual medicine or placebo pills? If so, how large is the difference between the two groups?

These are the kinds of questions that Chapter 3 explores in detail. They will also be followed up in later chapters, especially in Chapters 5 and 6.

Chapter 4 takes us into the world of making inferences beyond the data we examine. We often have data on only a small subset of all the possible units we are interested in. We call this our sample. The population, however, refers to all the possible and often unknown units of interest. Inferential statistics is mainly about making valid inferences or generalizations from samples to the broader populations, and Chapter 4 will guide us through the particulars.

Chapter 5 is an extension of Chapter 3, exploring how multiple independent variables might simultaneously affect one dependent variable. In this regard, unless I specify otherwise, I use "affect" and "is associated with" synonymously in Chapters 3–5. That said, the latter is the most accurate although both get the point across.

Chapter 6, building directly on Chapter 5, scrutinizes how to isolate the so-called causal effect of one specific independent variable on a dependent variable. If we can pull that off, we might be justified in using the term "affect" rather than "is associated with." More on this in Chapter 6.

If this is your first dance with statistical thinking, I promise that Chapters 2–6 will make you more capable as a statistical analyst. These new skills come in handy when we dive into Chapter 7. Here, we'll tackle some of the hurdles that pop up in statistical research, especially as it typically is presented in current affairs. Spoiler alert! Lots can go sideways from the collection of data and the crunching of numbers to the interpretation and the presentation of results. But no worries, we'll be navigating all of that together.

Finally, Chapter 8 puts all the pieces together and applies everything we have learned in the earlier chapters into a real-life statistical research setting. In other words, I'll be walking the talk, putting into practice all the key points I have been preaching throughout the first seven chapters of the book.

The questions mentioned a few paragraphs back give you a hint of the teaching approach I use in the book. Instead of explaining statistical concepts in abstract terms or using fictional data, I follow the path of explaining via recognizable daily-life examples and by using real-life data. Plus, I have peppered the book with four case studies that will be revisited and build upon from chapter to chapter.

At the end of each chapter, you will find the key learning points, the chapter notes, and the further reading suggestions. The notes provide references and delve into the technical and/or nice-to-know details that I for reasons of keeping things as easy as possible have omitted from the main text. I'm a big fan of the renowned physicist Richard P. Feynman's teaching philosophy: "If you cannot explain something in simple terms, **you** don't understand it."

KEY LEARNING POINTS

The key learning points in this chapter were:

- Practical statistical analysis is not about memorizing formulas, doing arithmetic calculations by hand, or solving abstract algebraic equations.
- Practical statistical analysis is not difficult in a technical sense.
- Statistical analysis is first and foremost an investigative tool.
- Statistical analysis questions are, or should be, driven by an inquisitive mode to find out things we previously did not know about.
- Statistical analyses are carried out on data, and such data normally refer to many numbers arranged in spreadsheet-like matrixes, as in rows and columns.
- The entities in the data rows are called units or observations.
- The columns in the data are called variables, and a variable's name normally appears on the top of a column.
- Variables have different measurement levels, and a fundamental distinction can be made between quantitative and categorical variables.
- The measurement level of a variable puts restrictions on how it may be analyzed statistically. For example, the mean or median requires that the variable in question is on the quantitative measurement level or can be "treated" as a variable on the quantitative measurement level.
- "Big data" are like "small data" but with more rows (units) and columns (variables).
- There are three main types of statistical (research) questions: descriptive, associational, and inferential.

NOTES

1 Gillham (2001) provides the authoritative biography of Galton. For shorter introductions to some of Galton's statistical endeavors, see Stanton (2001) and Kennedy-Shafer (2024).

2 Galton collected data on 481 adult sons and 453 adult daughters. For the sake of simplifying the presentation, I examine only the sons to avoid the complication of scaling the daughters' height with a factor of 1.08 (as Galton did).

3 Quantitative variables may be subdivided into continuous or discrete variables. The former can be any type of number (e.g., -3.17, 0.56, 6, $100,138.457$), whereas the latter refer to whole numbers (integers) such as number of nights stayed in a hospital (e.g., $0, 1, 2, \ldots$) and goals scored in football. The distinction between continuous and discrete might be important for some applications in more advanced statistical analysis, but I won't delve into these in this introductory book.

4 See Békés and Kézdi (2021, pp. 22–24).

5 For reasons that are followed up in Chapter 3, I try to avoid claiming that one variable "is related to" or "interrelated with" another variable. But the general meaning is synonymous.

FURTHER READING

As further reading on the most important topics of this chapter, I recommend Bailor and Pennington (2023), Spiegelhalter (2019), Stigler (2016), and Wheelan (2014). I also recommend these four books to follow up the contents of the upcoming Chapters 2 and 3.

DESCRIBING VARIABLES

CHAPTER OVERVIEW

DOI: 10.4324/9781032640808-2

INTRODUCTION

Statistical analysis is our detective tool for answering (research) questions. The answers we seek are buried in the heap of numbers called data. So, statistical analysis is an inquisitive tool to simplify the information on variables in a data set. This simplification process involves crunching the units' scores on a variable – say, the number of nights stayed in a hospital, or adult sons' height in inches – into a summary measure. A primary objective is to paint a broad picture, as in *describing* in the aggregate.

Variable description concerns three interrelated tasks: (1) figuring out about central tendency (what is typical for a variable), (2) getting a grip on statistical variation (a variable's dispersion), and (3) understanding statistical distribution (a variable's visual characteristics). This chapter covers the ins and outs of these three tasks.

Questions of central tendency are what-is-typical questions: what is typical for a variable? We have already met the two main measures of central tendency: the *average* and the *median*. We often use the term *mean* for the average, and I'll use both. The third measure of central tendency is the *mode*. When we want to find out about what is typical for a variable in our data, we tell our statistics program to compute the mean, the median, or the mode – or all three of them if we are very eager. Let's dig deeper into these measures in the context of football (or soccer for my American readers) as a backdrop.

CENTRAL TENDENCY: GOAL-SCORING IN FOOTBALL

The first question we examine by statistical analysis is about goal-scoring. How many goals does a player in a top-tier football league typically score in a season? This question will be answered for a data set that includes the 310 outfield players in the top-tier Norwegian league for the 2022 season.[1]

Let's get the ball rolling!

Our first approach is to find the average or mean of the goal-scoring variable. To do so, we start by adding up the goals scored by player number one, player number two, and so on, right up to player number 310. We then divide that total by 310. Well, to be precise, we tell our statistics program to do that for us. Formally (and at times I must be formal, but I promise to keep it to a minimum), if we let the symbol y represent the goal-scoring variable, we find the mean of y, denoted $\bar{y}$, by the formula:

$$\bar{y} = \frac{\sum y_i}{n},$$

where $\sum$ is the summation sign for the goals scored by the individual players, y_i, and n is the number of players (units) in the data.[2] No matter how you slice it, my statistics program calculates the mean or average for the goal-scoring variable to be 2.37. The first answer to our first research question is that a typical football player scores 2.37 goals in a season.

Our second approach is to find the median of the goal-scoring variable. By arranging the 310 players in ascending order according to the number of goals they scored, we find the median in the middle of this distribution. The so-called *frequency table* is instrumental here, and it is displayed in Table 2.1.

Table 2.1 Frequency table for goal-scoring variable. N = 310

Number of goals	Frequency	Frequency in percent	Cumulative percent
0	94	30.32	30.32
1	66	21.29	51.61
2	57	18.39	70.00
3	23	7.42	77.42
4	22	7.10	84.52
5	14	4.52	89.03
6	8	2.58	91.61
7	5	1.61	93.23
8	4	1.29	94.52
9	5	1.61	96.13
10	1	0.32	96.45
11	2	0.65	97.10
12	2	0.65	97.74
13	1	0.32	98.06
14	1	0.32	98.39
15	3	0.97	99.35
16	1	0.32	99.68
25	1	0.32	100

Table 2.1 shows the frequency distribution of goals scored for the 2022 season. About 30 percent of the players, or 94 players to be exact, did not score any goals. On the other end of the spectrum, one player, the top goal scorer, managed to net 25 goals. To find the median, we look at the cumulative percentage column on the right-hand side of the table. We already know that 30 percent of the players did not score any goals (second row). The third row tells us that just over half of the players – 51.61 percent to be exact – scored either zero or one goal. So, the player smack in the middle of the goal-scoring distribution scored one goal. This is the median. The second answer to our question is that the typical player scores one goal in a season.

The mean and the median often provide roughly the same answer to the question of what is typical for a variable, like they did for the patient data back in Chapter 1. If that is the case, we are free to choose between the two measures when we report our findings. But in the present case, the mean (2.37) and the median (1) are not equal by far. The distinction between mean and median mentioned in Chapter 1 now gets relevant. The mean is the average number of goals scored in the data, while the median is the number of goals scored by the average player in the data.[3] Why, then, are these measures so different? I'm sure you have already figured it out. About 30 percent of the players did not score at all in the season, and 89 percent scored five goals or less. On the other hand, nine players managed to score twelve goals or more. These high-scoring players pull the mean of scoring upward and away from the median of scoring. As a corollary, this implies that the mean is more sensitive to extreme values in the data than the median. By the way, we call such extreme values *outliers* in statistical lingo.

Imagine adding a player scoring a mind-blowing 200 goals to the data set. The mean of the scoring variable would then jump to three goals. The median, in contrast, would be unaffected; it would not bat an eyelid and remain at one goal. The kicker is that both the mean and the median answer what-is-typical questions. Sometimes they give roughly the same answer, and sometimes they do not. When they do differ, we should dig deeper in our data to find out what is causing the discrepancy.

The mode gives us the third answer to the question of what is typical for a variable. The definition of the mode is simple: the most frequent value a variable takes on. Table 2.1 already gives the answer for our goal-scoring case: zero goals. The largest group of the players, or 30 percent of the players, have this value. If we must pick just one value from all possible values a variable may take on as our answer to the question of what is most typical, we would choose the mode. That mode is zero goals in the present case.

STATISTICAL VARIATION: GOAL-SCORING IN FOOTBALL

The second task of variable description concerns getting a grip of variables' variation. (Some use the terms statistical dispersion or spread, but I'll stick to variation.) Questions on statistical variation are to-what-extent questions. To what extent are the units located close to the mean; to what extent are the units located far away from the mean? We mainly use four measures to quantify such variation: the *range*, the *interquartile range* (IQR), the *standard deviation* (SD), and the *coefficient of variation* (CV).

Table 2.1 tells us about both the range and the IQR of the goal-scoring variable. The range is the difference between the highest (largest) and lowest (smallest) value a variable may take on. This range is 25 for the goal-scoring variable: $25 - 0 = 25$. A potential problem with the range as a measure of variation is its dependence on extreme values. To understand why, let's leave out the top-scorer (25 goals) from the data. The range now became 16, since the runner-up scored 16 goals in total. The IQR sidesteps this problem by measuring the range for the middle 50 percent of players in the scoring distribution. This is the difference between zero and three goals in Table 2.1. The IQR, measuring the range for the middle 50 percent of units in a variable's distribution, is three goals for these football player data.

The range and IQR tell us how the values of a variable spread out around its mean. But the most important measure of such variation is the SD. Here is the idea. Some of the players scored three goals, while others scored five or nine. The deviation or distance for the five-goal scorers to the overall mean ($5 - 2.37 = 2.63$) is thus larger than the deviation for the three-goal scorers ($3 - 2.37 = 0.63$). And since goals scored are always whole numbers (integers), all players *must* have some deviation from the mean of 2.37. The average or mean deviation in this regard is what we call the SD or s.

We get the SD by taking the square root of something called the *variance* or s^2. The formula to get the variance (sorry!), if we once more let the goal-scoring variable be symbolized by y, is:

$$s^2 = \frac{\sum(y_i - \overline{y})^2}{n - 1},$$

where, again, $\sum$ is the summation sign for the goals scored by the individual players, y_i, $\overline{y}$ is the mean of y, and n is the number of players (units) in the data.[4] According to my trusty statistics program, the SD or s for our goal-scoring variable is about 3.22. The SD measures the variation around the mean: the larger the SD, the further away from the mean the typical unit tends to be located. In other words, a larger SD suggests there is more variation.

The fourth measure of variation is the CV. The CV is the SD of y divided by its mean ($\overline{y}$), all multiplied by 100. So, for the goal-scoring variable, we get: $(3.22/2.37) \times 100 = 135.86$. Both the SD and the CV have limited interest if we are looking at only *one* variable in *one* data set. But they really come into play when we are comparing one variable to another, or when comparing different subgroups in the data with respect to one variable. More on this later in the chapter; stay tuned!

STATISTICAL DISTRIBUTION: GALTON'S SONS AND GOAL-SCORING IN FOOTBALL

The third task of variable description is about the understanding of statistical distributions. Questions of distribution may be thought of as what-does-a-variable-look-like questions: what does the distribution of y look like in a visual sense? Let's circle back to Galton's data for a brief moment. The distribution for the height of the sons is shown in the *histogram* in Figure 2.1. (For reference, the mean or average height is 69.2 inches or about 176 centimeters. The median height is also 69.2 inches.)

A histogram effectively shows the physical shape of a variable: the height of the bars (aka bins) tells us how many units (here: sons) there are in each bar. So, the taller the bar, the more units there are "inside" it. This suggests that most of Galton's sons were about 70 inches, as per the tallest bar.

The *bar chart* is the histogram's cousin, used when dealing with a variable that has fewer potential integer values – like the number of nights someone stays in a hospital, or the number of goals scored in football. The bar chart in Figure 2.2 shows the distribution of our goal-scoring variable. We notice that the tallest bar corresponds to zero goals, something we already knew from Table 2.1. Both bar charts and histograms are, at their core, just visual representations of a frequency table.

One difference between Figure 2.1 (the Galton data) and Figure 2.2 (the football data) is striking. While the height variable in Galton's data has a *symmetrical* shape around its average value, the scoring variable in the football data has no such thing. No, the scoring variable has a *right skew*. For right-skewed variables, the mean (2.37 goals) is usually larger than the median (1 goal), which in turn is larger than the mode (zero goals): mean > median > mode. We have the opposite for left-skewed variables. The mode is larger than the median, which in turn is larger than the mean: mode > median > mean. Things are most often simpler for symmetrical distributions. The mean, the median, and the mode are generally close most of the time: mean ≈ median ≈ mode.

One distribution is of vital importance, if not to say a game-changer, in statistics: the Gaussian or *normal* distribution.

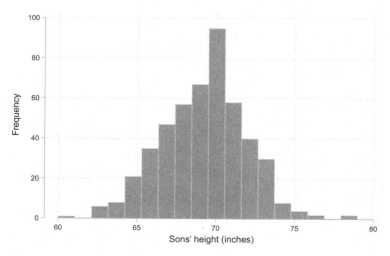

Figure 2.1 Histogram of sons' height in Galton's data

I have overlaid the normal distribution on Galton's height variable in Figure 2.3. Galton's height variable is not perfectly normally distributed, but it comes rather close for all intents and purposes.

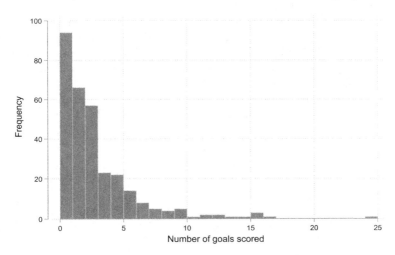

Figure 2.2 Bar chart of the variable goal-scoring in football

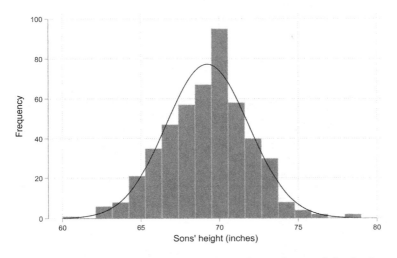

Figure 2.3 Histogram of sons' height in Galton's data, with normal distribution
            superimposed

The upshot? For a normally distributed variable, we always know, without doing any actual calculations, that the mean, the median, and the mode are *exactly* equal. I have more to say on the normal distribution in Chapter 4.

Several types of plots may show a statistical distribution and compare it with a normal distribution. The *Kernel plot,* or Kernel density plot, is an equivalent of the histogram with a smoother visual appearance. This is shown in Figure 2.4. Again, we note the similarity with the normal distribution.

Table 2.2 sums up the purposes of descriptive statistical analysis along with some of the main concepts typically used.

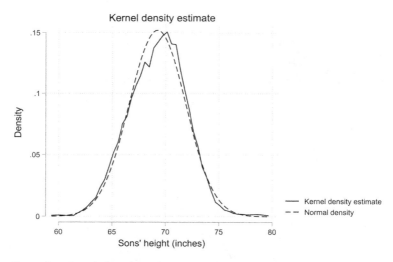

Figure 2.4 Kernel plot of sons' height in Galton's data, with normal distribution superimposed

Table 2.2 Purposes of descriptive statistical analysis and its main concepts

	The purpose is to find out about:		
	Central tendency	Variation	Distribution
Main concepts	Mean	Range/IQR	Histograms
	Median	Standard deviation	Bar charts
	Mode	Coefficient of variation	Kernel plots

INTERLUDE: VARIABLES' MEASUREMENT LEVEL ONCE MORE

So far in this chapter, we have kind of assumed that all variables are quantitative – like height in inches or the number of goals scored in a football match. But let's be real, that is a bit of a stretch. Plenty of real-life variables are categorical. We usually divide these categorical variables into two main types: nominal variables or ordinal variables. (Alternatively, we say that a variable is on the nominal or the ordinal measurement level.) Nominal variables are this-or-that variables with no ranking, like biological sex (male or female), football player position (goalkeeper, defender, midfielder, winger, striker), or day of the week. For an ordinal variable, in contrast, there is a ranking or order among the alternatives the variable may take on. A classic example is the Likert-scale, where people must totally disagree, disagree, neither disagree nor agree, agree, or totally agree with some statement. Such evaluation involves ranking, where totally agreeing obviously is *more in* agreement than just agreeing or disagreeing. But there are no quantifiable or "fixed" distances between the alternatives, as in the case of the quantitative variables. We take a quick look into such non-quantitative variables below.

WHAT IS TYPICAL? NOMINAL VARIABLES

For a nominal variable, the what-is-typical question boils down to the mode and the frequency table we saw in Table 2.1. We can also whip up a bar chart of a nominal variable. Table 2.3 and Figure 2.5 exemplify these two alternative approaches for the player position variable in our football data.

The mode, as in the most frequent alternIative or widest horizontal bar, is defender. The percentage is 36. So, if you were to pick

Table 2.3 Frequency table for the variable player position. N = 310

Player position	Frequency	Frequency in percent	Cumulative percent
Defender	113	36.45	36.45
Midfielder	89	28.71	65.16
Winger	59	19.03	84.19
Striker	49	15.81	100

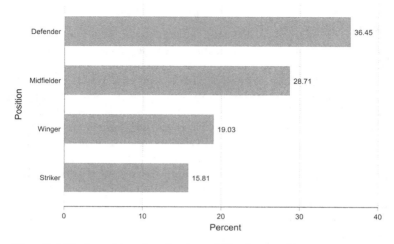

Figure 2.5 Horizontal bar chart for the variable player position

a footballer at random from the data, there is a good chance your guy plays defense.

WHAT IS TYPICAL? ORDINAL VARIABLES

Now, let's shift our attention to a fresh data set. The units are 468 Norwegian wine club members.[5] The variables are a set of questions asked in a member survey. (We call our units *respondents* when analyzing data on people having answered a survey questionnaire.) The age distribution for the wine club members is depicted in Figure 2.6. We notice that most members are between roughly 45 and 75 years old, as per the tallest bars in the middle of the age distribution. I can also inform you that the mean age is 58 years.

Let's zoom in on the Likert-statement, "I often discuss wine with my family, friends, and colleagues." The answer categories to this statement were totally disagree, disagree, neither disagree nor agree, agree, or totally agree, with codings in the data from 0 (totally disagree) to 4 (totally agree). The frequency table for this *ordinal* variable is presented in Table 2.4.

The most common answer – the mode – is agreeing. This answer applies to almost 42 percent of the members. We find the wine club

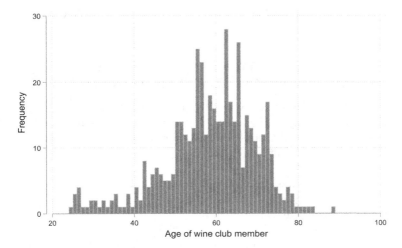

Figure 2.6 Histogram of wine club members' age

Table 2.4 Frequency table for wine statement variable. N = 468

Wine statement[a]	Frequency	Frequency in percent	Cumulative percent
Totally disagree	4	0.85	0.85
Disagree	33	7.05	7.91
Neither/nor ...	74	15.81	23.72
Agree	196	41.88	65.60
Totally agree	161	34.40	100

[a] The statement reads, "I often discuss wine with my family, friends, and colleagues."

members to be on the agreeing side of the Likert-statement, much as expected. Now, many analysts think of ordinal variables like this one as "almost" quantitative with values from 0 to 4, albeit being aware of that this is technically incorrect. Why do they think like that? Because it lets them work out means and medians. For these data, these values are 3.02 (mean) and 3.0 (median). The upshot is that we sometimes answer what-is-typical questions for ordinal variables by calculating means and medians.

Below I introduce four case studies to illuminate the topics covered so far in this chapter: mean, median, mode, range, IQR, SD, CV, and variable distributions. I also promise to add some new graphs into the mix. As mentioned, we return to these case studies in later chapters in the book.

CASE STUDY 1: THE TYPICAL QUANTITATIVE CHARACTERISTICS OF PIZZA RESTAURANT MEALS

Picture yourself stopping every 11th guest leaving a pizza restaurant from a big chain and conducting a quick interview. Imagine also that you kept on doing this until you had interviewed 300 guests. You ask them the following five questions:

1   How much was the total bill for you and your fellow diners' meal?
2   How many diners were you in total?
3   How many individual orders did the meal include?
4   How much (if anything) did you and your fellow diners tip in total?
5   Were any alcoholic beverages ordered in conjunction with the meal?

Well, you can stop imagining because I have collected a real data set containing the answers to these five questions or variables for 300 restaurant guests or units: In short, I have a data set consisting of 300 units and five variables. Let's don our inquisitive glasses and dig into the typical characteristics of these variables. The central tendency and statistical variation measures – the "descriptive statistics" in the lingo – for the first four variables are presented in condensed form in Table 2.5. Similarly, the descriptive statistics for the fifth (nominal) variable are shown in Table 2.6.

Table 2.5 Descriptive statistics for pizza restaurant meal data. N = 300

	Mean	Median	Min	Max	IQR	SD	CV
Total bill	523	455	105	2,298	316	319	61
Number of diners	2.5	2	1	12	1	1.5	60
Number of orders	5.7	5	1	22	4	3.5	61
Total tip	12.5	0	0	172	16	23	184

Note. Total bill and total tip are in Norwegian Krone (NOK). NOK 100 has traditionally been the equivalent of roughly €10 or $11.

Table 2.6 Frequency table for alcoholic beverage question in pizza restaurant meal data. N = 300

Question[a]	Frequency	Frequency in percent	Cumulative percent
No	206	69	69
Yes	94	31	100

[a] The question was, "Were any alcoholic beverages bought in conjunction with the meal?" Codings are 0 (No) and 1 (Yes).

On top of Table 2.5, we see that the average total bill for a pizza restaurant meal is NOK 523 or about €52 or $48. The median is a bit less: NOK 455. The range for the total bill variable is NOK 2,193 (2,298 − 105 = 2,193), while the IQR − the range covering the 50 percent of meals in the middle of the total bill distribution − is NOK 316. Lastly, the SD is NOK 319, and the CV is 61 ((319/523) × 100 ≈ 61).

Figure 2.7 combines the information on the median and the IQR for the total bill variable, and it is called a *box and whisker plot*. The horizontal line in the middle of the box is the median: NOK 455. The box itself contains 50 percent of the meals, and the vertical distance from the top to the bottom of the box is the IQR: NOK 316. The whiskers are the two horizontal lines that extend from

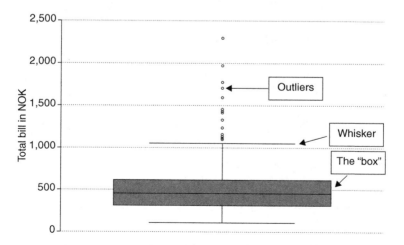

Figure 2.7 Box and whisker plot of total bill for meal (in Norwegian Krone)

the box. In practice, all bills fall within the price range between the upper and lower whisker. The hollow dots are the outliers. These are meals with much higher total bills than the rest of the meals.

Table 2.5 also reveals that the average dining party included two plus persons (mean = 2.5; median = 2). Yet while some people dined solo, others were part of a group of 12. The average meal included almost six individual orders, ranging from just 1 all the way up to 22. Finally, there is a large difference between the mean and the median for the total tip variable. The mean is NOK 12.5, but the median is zero – as in no tip. Since the mean is much larger than the median, we have a right-skewed distribution. From this we may deduce that a large percentage of the meals did not include a tip. The histogram in Figure 2.8 confirms this, showing that more than half of the 300 meals (55 percent) did not come with a tip. This high proportion of not providing a tip, aka stiffing, is explained by the fact that tipping is far from mandatory in Norway.

Table 2.6 lays out the descriptive statistics for the alcoholic beverage variable. Thirty-one percent of the meals included some form of alcoholic beverage. Later in the book, we'll continue with this case study, asking other kinds of tasteful questions. Now, let's change gears and take a peek at some other case study data.

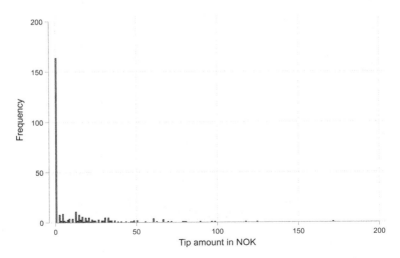

Figure 2.8 Histogram of tip amount variable

CASE STUDY 2: WOMEN'S SPRINT BIATHLON IN THE OLYMPICS

In women's sprint event in biathlon, skiers kick off with a 2.5-km ski lap before shooting five times in the lying position. For every missed shot they must complete a 150-m penalty lap before they can enter the second 2.5-km lap, ending with a shouting bout (of five shots) in the prone position. Then follows a second penalty lap procedure before the third and final 2.5-km lap to the finish line. The athlete with the fastest race time from start to finish, including the time spent on shooting and penalty laps, wins the race.

Our data cover the women's sprint biathlon event for the six Olympic winter games from 2002 and onward: 2002, 2006, 2010, 2014, 2018, and 2022. The data encompass 501 individual race performances or units. (The number of skiers is not 501 because many skiers took part in several games.) Table 2.7 presents descriptive statistics for the variables total race time in minutes and number of hits on target based on all ten shots.

Table 2.7 Descriptive statistics for women's sprint biathlon in six Olympic winter games. N = 501

	Mean	*Median*	*Min*	*Max*	*IQR*	*SD*	*CV*
Panel A							
Race time: 2002	23.61	23.21	20.69	30.25	2.05	1.81	7.65
Race time: 2006	25.17	24.60	22.52	33.87	2.33	1.95	7.75
Race time: 2010	22.04	22.09	19.93	25.40	1.60	1.17	5.31
Race time: 2014	23.17	22.99	21.11	27.62	1.84	1.37	5.91
Race time: 2018	23.41	23.33	21.10	26.42	1.77	1.20	5.13
Race time: 2022	23.32	23.27	20.74	26.46	1.48	1.17	5.02
Panel B							
Hits: 2002	7.97	8	2	10	2	1.56	19.57
Hits: 2006	8.16	9	2	10	2	1.53	18.80
Hits: 2010	8.20	8	5	10	2	1.34	16.34
Hits: 2014	8.31	9	4	10	1	1.35	16.25
Hits: 2018	7.48	8	3	10	2	1.51	20.19
Hits: 2022	8.13	8	5	10	2	1.26	15.50

The average race time for the 2002 games clocked in at 23.61 minutes. (23.50 minutes is 23 minutes and 30 seconds.) The median of 23.21 minutes was close to the mean. The winner of the race spent 20.69 minutes from start to finish (Min column), while the skier finishing last spent 30.25 minutes (Max column). The range is the difference between these extremes: 30.25−20.69 = 9.56 minutes. The results for statistical variation were 2.05 (IQR), 1.81 (SD), and 7.65 (CV). Comparing the 2002 results with the performances in later games, we observe no clear trend for the mean or median race times. In contrast, and apart from the 2014 games, there is a tendency toward decreasing CVs with time. This tightening-around-the-mean for race time might be thought of as tougher competition in more recent Olympic winter games.

In 2002, the skiers hit the target 7.97 times out of ten in total on average. The median was eight hits. Some skiers hit only two targets (Min), whereas some hit all ten (Max). The IQR, SD, and CV were, respectively, 2.0, 1.56, and 19.57. Comparing the 2002 results with the performances in later games, we again observe no distinct trend for mean or median performance. Save for the 2018 games, we may nevertheless have a trend toward lower CVs for the shooting performances. If so, this might be a sign of fiercer competition in more recent games.

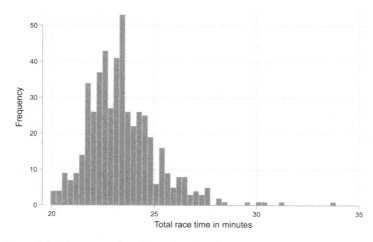

Figure 2.9 Histogram of total race time in minutes

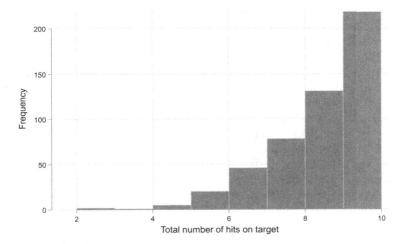

Figure 2.10 Bar chart of total number of hits on target

The distributions for the two variables, combined for all games, appear in Figures 2.9 and 2.10. We observe some resemblance with the normal distribution for the race time variable. In contrast, the shooting variable has a severe left skew. Not surprisingly, we'll take a new shot on these case study data in later chapters.

So far, we have been focusing on analyzing one variable at a time. This is known in the lingo as (doing) *univariate* analysis, and much descriptive analyses are carried out in this way. But we can also analyze two variables at the same time. This is called (doing) *bivariate* analysis. In other words, we can compare means, medians, measures of variation, and variable distributions for two or more *subgroups* in our data. For the two remaining case studies in this chapter, I introduce such subgroup or category comparison. More − much more! − on this in Chapter 3.

CASE STUDY 3: THE PRICE, QUALITY RATING, AND ALCOHOL CONTENT OF BEERS

Just like in many other countries, you can pick up a bottle of beer from regular grocery stores in Norway. But if you want a beer with an alcohol content higher than 4.75 percent, you only get this one in state–run outlets known as "Vinmonopolet." Table 2.8 presents descriptive statistics for 462 such bottles of beer (0.33 liter) or units available through Vinmonopolet.[6]

The beers are priced between NOK 29 and NOK 333, with an average cost of NOK 89 and a median of NOK 68. The IQR, the SD, and the CV are, respectively, 47.27, 54.13, and 60.73. The quality rating variable is the Parker scale, a popular tool for judging the taste of alcoholic beverages. It ranges from 50 points (undrinkable) to 100 points (perfection). The average beer in the data falls on the higher end of the scale, with a mean score of 86.60 points and a median of 87 points. And while the worst-tasting beer gets a score of 74 points, the best-tasting beer scores 94. This gives us the range of 20 points. The middle 50 percent of beers have a range – or IQR – of four points. Lastly, the alcohol content of the beers varies from 4.8 to 15 percent, with a mean of 7.80 percent and a median of 7 percent.

One crucial detail about the beer data is not shown in Table 2.8, namely that the beers stem from two production countries: Sweden ($n = 135$) or the USA ($n = 327$). These are two *subgroups* in the data. Figure 2.11 is a box and whisker plot showing the beer bottle prices broken down by country of production.

There are a couple of things worth noting about Figure 2.11, in which the medians are represented by the two horizontal lines in the middle of each box. The median price is higher for US beers (NOK 81) than for Swedish beers (NOK 63). And, if we look at the vertical length of the boxes and the distance between the whiskers, we can see that there is a wider price range among US beers.

A *violin plot* is sort of a hybrid, combining elements of a box and whisker plot and a Kernel density plot. Figure 2.12 presents this plot for the beer price variable, split by country of production. The dots in the black rectangles (representing the middle 50 percent of beers)

Table 2.8 Descriptive statistics for beer data. N = 462

	Mean	Median	Min	Max	IQR	SD	CV
Price per bottle	89.13	68.41	29.09	333.07	47.27	54.13	60.73
Quality rating	86.60	87	74	95	4	3.28	3.79
Alcohol content (%)	7.80	7	4.8	15	3	2.39	30.64

Note. Price per bottle (0.33 liter) is in Norwegian Krone (NOK). NOK 100 has traditionally been the equivalent of roughly €10 or $11.

are the medians. Once again, we see that the typical US beer tends to be pricier than the typical Swedish beer. The price variation is also much more compressed among the Swedish beers.

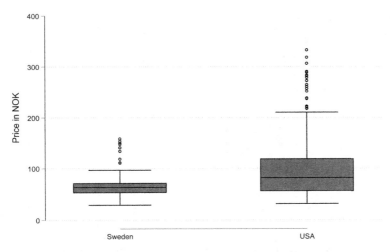

Figure 2.11 Box and whisker plot of price per beer bottle, by production country

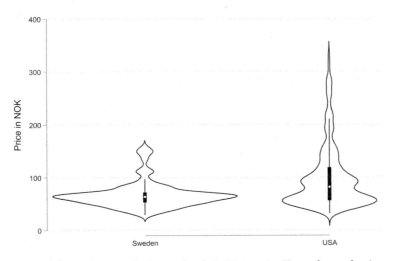

Figure 2.12 Violin plot of price per bottle in Norwegian Krone, by production country

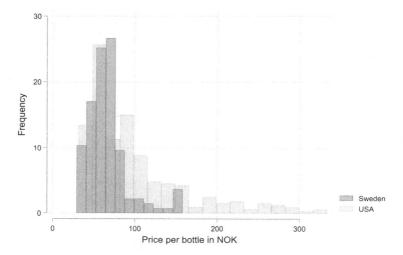

Figure 2.13 Histogram of price per beer bottle, by production country

It is sometimes illuminating to break down distributions by sub-groups in the data. Figure 2.13 does just that for the beer price variable. The distribution for US beers extends further to the right than that for Swedish beers. This lines up with what we saw in Figures 2.11 and 2.12.

CASE STUDY 4: THE WELL-BEING OF NORWEGIANS

Level-of-living surveys are common. The goal of such surveys, typically conducted among thousands of adults, is to get information about the well-being of a country's residents. Level-of-living surveys have historically been questionnaires to be filled out at home, but in recent years phone or email surveys have taken over. About 7,500 persons were interviewed in the most recent round of the Norwegian level-of-living survey in 2019. You can think of these respondents as a micro-cosmos – or a miniature model, if you prefer – of the total Norwegian adult population. (We return to the concepts of populations and samples more formally in Chapter 4.)

One question in the survey read, "How satisfied are you with your life?" The answer categories to this question ranged from "not satisfied at all" (coded 0) to "very satisfied" (coded 10). I refer to this variable as subjective well-being. And because this ordinal variable has 11 ranked categories, I treat it as if it were quantitative. The mean is 8.11, and the median is 8 for the 6,539 adults aged between 18 and 70 years, to which I restrict the analysis. So, it seems like the typical Norwegian adult is pretty pleased with his or her life in general.

While the typical Norwegian might be a happy fellow, it is not a leap to suggest that the mean and median of subjective well-being might vary among different subgroups in the data, like men versus women and younger people versus older people. A third classification concerns differences in health level status, which also was a survey topic. Respondents had to assess their general health as either poor, ok, good, or very good. The so-called *dot plot* in Figure 2.14 breaks down the mean of subjective well-being on these four health level statuses and the biological sex of the respondent in a purely descriptive manner.

There are a couple of things to note about Figure 2.14. First, the mean scores of comparable men and women are located almost exactly on the same vertical spots across the board; there is virtually no difference between the sexes when it comes to subjective well-being. Second, and in contrast, we find large differences in

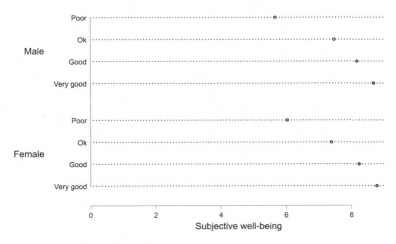

Figure 2.14 Subjective well-being by health level status and biological sex of respondents

subjective well-being based on perceived health levels: the better the health, the higher the subjective well-being.

DESCRIPTIVE STATISTICS AS THE INTRODUCTION TO BIVARIATE ANALYSIS

The results covered in this chapter might be considered intriguing on their own, especially in applied settings where what-is-typical questions often are important. In most research settings, however, describing data is usually a getting-to-know-your-data phase before the main event or the finals: exploring variable *associations*. Studying such associations is the topic of the next chapter.

KEY LEARNING POINTS

The key learning points in this chapter were:

- Variable description is all about finding the central tendency (mean, median, and mode), the variation (range, IQR, SD, and CV), and the visual distribution of a variable.
- Variables may be described in tables or in graphs (plots/charts).
- Variables are on different measurement levels. For practical purposes, the most important levels are the quantitative level, the ordinal level, and the nominal level.
- A variable's measurement determines what kind of statistical questions can be asked about it. Variables on the quantitative measurement level have fewest restrictions in this regard.
- The central tendency, variation, and distribution of a variable may be broken down on subgroups in the data and presented in tables or in graphs (plots/charts).
- In most research settings, describing variables is often the first step toward the study of variable associations.

NOTES

1 I use these football player data throughout the book. Thanks again to Amund Lillejordet and Espen Kletthagen Stensby for the permission to do so. You find more extensive analyses of these data in Thrane (2024a, 2024b).

2 The summation operator (Σ) is a kind of shorthand that tells you to add up all the "numbers" that come after it. Formally in statistics, we use Latin letters to refer to samples and Greek letters to refer to populations (both terms to be defined in Chapter 4). But since such formalism is exactly the stuff taking focus away from what data analysis is about (and what makes it unnecessary complicated for many of us), I'm not going to stick rigidly to this notation in the book. For instance, when I refer to samples in tables, I use "N" to describe the number of units, although "n" is more technically correct.

3 See Bailor and Pennington (2023).

4 We divide by $n - 1$ whenever we consider the data to be a sample from some (much larger) population; cf. endnote 2 above. In practice, this has no consequences whatsoever when we are dealing with large samples.

5 You find a more extensive analysis of these data in Thrane (2019).

6 These beers are a subset of the data analyzed in Thrane et al. (2024).

FURTHER READING

In addition to the books mentioned as suggested further reading in Chapter 1, I recommend Agresti (2018), Freedman et al. (2007), and Thrane (2022) as follow-ups to this chapter.

EXAMINING ASSOCIATIONS BETWEEN TWO VARIABLES

Bivariate analysis

CHAPTER OVERVIEW

DOI: 10.4324/9781032640808-3

INTRODUCTION

Many of us use phrases like "things are related" in everyday conversation. What are we really saying when using such expressions? I have no crystal-clear answer for this, sorry. But generally, it seems to me that we by observation or indirect experience often have learned that when event A occurs, so does event B. Or less extreme: whenever A occurs, B *tends* to occur. The classic example is lightening followed by thunder. Or when lots of hours preparing for an exam result in a success on the exam in question.

But there are no things in statistics, only variables. We also prefer the term *associated with* rather than *related to*; we claim that variables are associated – or that they might be. Recall how Chapter 1 mentioned that the independent variable affected the dependent variable in the sense that this was assumed. Well, from now on, I'll be referring to the independent variable as x and the dependent variable as y. Any statistical association implies that when x increases or decreases, so does y – as in more often than not. If y does not appear to increase or decrease due to a change in x, we say that x and y are not related. Or not associated, to be notoriously precise.

Associational research questions are the bread and butter of modern statistical analysis in research settings. Sure, describing variables one by one, as we did in Chapter 2, is important in the same way a qualification round is. But at the end of the day, or in the finals if you prefer, statistical associations nevertheless make the headlines. These statistical associations occupy the driver's seat in this chapter.

Let's go back to Galton's data for a recap, where I have set up Figure 1.2 as Figure 3.1. We could say that fathers' and sons' stature are related; that there is a relationship between the two variables. But from now on, we'll mainly be talking in terms of variable associations. What is the main takeaway from the association in the figure? The answer, if we read from left to right (as we should), is an upward sloping trend line. This implies a *positive* association between the variables: an increase in fathers' height entails an increase in sons' height. Or more precisely, taller fathers tend to have taller sons more often than shorter fathers. And vice versa, shorter fathers tend to have shorter sons more often than taller fathers.

The variable association in Figure 3.1 is positive. But such variable associations can also be *negative*. A negative association between

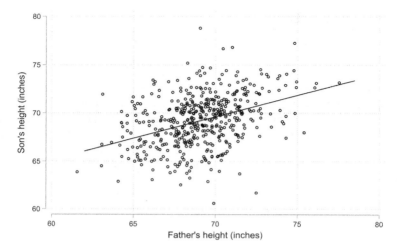

Figure 3.1 Scatterplot of Galton's data, with general trend line

x and y implies a downward sloping trend line. Or x and y might not be associated at all. What kind of trend line would that suggest? Yep, you got it right. A horizontal trend line suggests no association between the variables in question. If you did not get it right, no worries. Everything will become crystal clear by the end of this chapter!

The first part of this chapter deals with associations between two quantitative variables, which is the most pedagogical place to start. This is Galton's home turf. The second part deals with associations in which the independent variable, x, is categorical. The third part covers the situation in which both x and y are categorical. Finally, the chapter closes with some "special" topics.

CORRELATION AND REGRESSION

We are literally kicking things off by revisiting our football data. Figure 3.2 shows the association between the variables age of player and the total number of matches played in career. We notice the resemblance with Figure 3.1: there is a positive association between the variables. On average, older players have played more matches in their careers than younger players – quite obviously, we might add. When associating two quantitative variables in statistics, we typically employ one of two related statistical techniques: correlation or regression. The scatterplot in Figure 3.2 visualizes both the correlation and the linear (straight) regression line for the variables age and total number of matches played. (By the way, the trend line in Figure 3.1? That was, yes, a regression line.)

Correlation and regression are two ways to quantify the association between two quantitative variables. Let's start with correlation and then move on to regression. If you compare Figures 3.1 and 3.2, you will see that the data points in Figure 3.2 are more tightly scattered around the regression line. The *correlation coefficient*, to simplify, measures this tightness around a linear regression line. The correlation coefficient for the data in Figure 3.2 is 0.88, while the correlation coefficient for the data in Figure 3.1 is 0.39. So, in this tightness-sense, the football data association is better described as linear than the Galton data association. You will find the formula to calculate the correlation coefficient in any textbook on statistics or with a quick search on Google.[1] (Just to be clear: I see no reason to provide this introductory book with

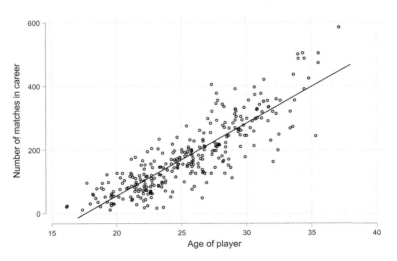

Figure 3.2 Scatterplot of total number of matches by age of player, with linear regression line

formulas that in any event are incomprehensible to most people. Plus, statistics programs are very much up to speed regarding all necessary formulas.)

A perfect positive correlation implies that all data points line up exactly *on* an upward sloping regression line. If that is the case, which never happens is in real life, the correlation coefficient is 1.00. A perfect negative correlation implies that all data points fall exactly on a downward sloping regression line. The correlation coefficient is then −1.00. In other words, most real-life correlation coefficients land somewhere in the interval between −0.90 and 0.90. And what about a correlation coefficient of 0.00? Yes, it means there is no linear association between the two variables.

That wraps up correlation. Regression is specifically concerned with the steepness of the regression line. Just how steeply does the line slope upward or downward? Or to what extent should the line more aptly be described as (close to) horizontal? The regression coefficient measures this steepness. A positive regression coefficient implies an upward sloping regression line; a negative regression coefficient implies a downward sloping regression line. So, a positive or negative regression coefficient suggests some kind of linear association between x and y. A regression coefficient of zero, in contrast, suggests an exact horizontal regression line, implying that x and y are not associated at all.

Some formalities might help us understand what the regression coefficient measures. Let's refer to the age of the football players as x and the total number of matches played as y. From your mathematical training, you might recall that any linear (regression) line can be characterized by the equation:

$$y = a + b \times x.$$

The b in this equation is the steepness of the line − or the regression coefficient in our lingo. (You might recognize this coefficient as the slope of the line, which means the exact same.) Simply put, the regression coefficient or slope expresses how much y changes when x increases by one unit. For our football data in Figure 3.2, this translates into:

Total number of football matches = a + b × age of player.

In this example, the regression coefficient is the change in the total number of matches played when a player's age increases by one year. Or more precisely, given that we are comparing players at the same point in time, the difference in the number of matches between a player who is, say, 25 years of age and a player who is 26. According to my statistics program, this regression coefficient is 22.90. When the variable player age goes up by one year, the variable total number of matches played goes up by almost 23 matches on average.[2] The two variables are certainly associated with each other.

The importance of the regression coefficient in modern statistical analysis cannot be overstated. The technical interpretation of this coefficient, b, is the change in y when x increases by one unit. The a in the regression equation is known as the constant.[3] This constant is the point where the regression line intersects the y-axis; it is the starting point of the regression line on the y-axis. Later on, we'll consider another aspect of this regression constant.

The last thing I want to touch on right now is R-squared or R^2. R^2 measures the extent to which the independent variable, x, explains the variation in the dependent variable, y. R^2 varies between zero and one, or between 0 and 100 percent. My statistics program calculates R^2 to be 0.78 or 78 percent for our football data regression. That means the age variable explains 78 percent of the variation in the total number of matches variable.[4] Results of regressions are often displayed in tables. Table 3.1 illustrates for our football regression shown in Figure 3.2.

The new feature in the table is the value of the constant: -403. This negative number suggests that the regression line starts below zero on the y-axis, as Figure 3.2 would show if the line were to be extended to the left.[5] But the star of regression is the b/slope/

Table 3.1 Total number of matches played by age of player. Linear regression

Independent variable	b
Age of player	23
Constant	−403
R^2	0.78
N	310

regression coefficient, which is 23 in our example. Having explained how correlation and regression work in a rudimentary manner, we are now ready to tackle more associational research questions. Let's revisit the case studies from Chapter 2. From this point on, however, I leave correlation behind as a pedagogical stepping-stone to regression, to focus on the latter. The appendix to this chapter clarifies some technical details of regression that might be worth a look before moving on. But no worries, this is not mandatory to get the basics of regression analysis in what follows in the upcoming case studies.

CASE STUDY 1: THE TYPICAL QUANTITATIVE CHARACTERISTICS OF PIZZA RESTAURANT MEALS, CONT.

Two of the variables in the pizza restaurant data are the total bill for the meal and the number of diners taking part in it. Since a larger group generally orders more food, we have reason to expect a positive association between these two quantitative variables. Hence, regression analysis fits the bill (pun totally intended!) for examining this research question.

Table 3.2 lays out the regression results, and Figure 3.3 shows the correlation and the regression line. At this point it is worth noting, though, that the figure does not include any information that is not already in the regression table. The regression coefficient is 125. This suggests that one more diner at the table increases the total bill by NOK 125 on average, in the sense that a four-person table pays NOK 125 more on average than a three-person table. We find, just as expected, a positive association between the two variables. The regression line would start at NOK 211

Table 3.2 Total bill for meal by number of diners. Linear regression

Independent variable	b	
Number of diners	125	
Constant	211	
R^2		0.36
N		300

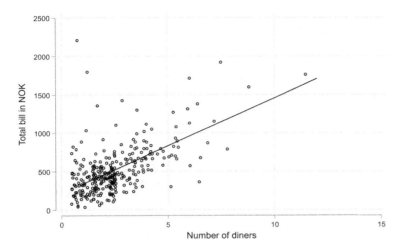

Figure 3.3 Scatterplot of total bill for meal and number of diners, with linear regression line

(the constant) if we were to extend it all the way to the y-axis.[6] And the number of diners accounts for 36 percent of the variation in the total bill variable (R^2).

CASE STUDY 2: WOMEN'S SPRINT BIATHLON IN THE OLYMPICS, CONT.

Given the way the biathlon sprint event is set up, we know that more missed shots in a race will add to the total race time: each missed shot results in a penalty lap before the skier may continue. This yields the expectation that the more targets hit, the better – as in *lower* – the total race time will be. My statistics program calculates the regression coefficient to be −0.64. We find a negative association between number of hits and total race time, just as expected. This association is shown in Figure 3.4. The interpretation of the regression coefficient is straightforward: on average, skiers hitting, say, eight targets have a race time that is about 0.64 minutes, or roughly 38 seconds, lower (faster) than skiers hitting seven targets. Just for the record, pun intended, none of the skiers hit fewer than two targets.

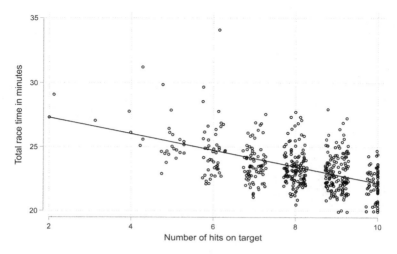

Figure 3.4 Scatterplot of total race time and number of hits on target, with linear regression line

WHEN THE INDEPENDENT VARIABLE, *X*, IS A CATEGORICAL VARIABLE

The independent variable, *x*, is categorical in many walks of life. But regression solves this case too. Let's go back to our football data. The dependent variable, *y*, is the total number of matches played in career (mean = 182; min = 10, max = 584; SD = 109). The independent variable, *x*, is whether a player has represented his national team or not. This *x*-variable is nominal and has two categories: no (coded 0) or yes (coded 1). Nominal variables having two categories are often called *dummy variables* or *dummies*.[7]

We want to find out if there is an association between the number of matches played variable and the national team representation variable. In the language of regression, this research question gets transformed into:

Total number of football matches = a + b × national team
representation.

In essence, we are just swapping the age variable we used earlier with the national team representation dummy. If I tell my statistics program to estimate this regression, I get:

Total number of football matches = 164 + 95 × national team representation.

The key here is to remember the interpretation of the regression coefficient: the change in y when x increases by one unit. In this example, the y is the total number of matches played, and the x is the national team dummy having two categories: not represented a national team = 0 or represented a national team = 1. With that in mind, we have the information we need. When x increases by one unit (as in comparing a player who has not represented his national team (coded 0) with one who has represented his team (coded 1)), the number of matches "increases" by 95 matches on average. In more succinct prose we say that, on average, national team players have played 95 more matches in their career than players with no national team representation. So, we surely witness an association between the two variables. After all, a difference of 95 matches is a far cry from a difference of zero matches.

The constant takes on a concrete and real-life interpretation in regressions where the x-variable is a dummy. To see how and why, we plug the two possible values for the national team dummy into the regression equation. For players with no representation for their national teams (coded 0), we get the prediction:

Total number of football matches = 164 + 95 × 0 →
164 + 0 = 164.

So, players with no representation for their national teams have played an average of 164 matches in their career. For players with representation for their national teams (coded 1), in contrast, we get the prediction:

Total number of football matches = 164 + 95 × 1 →
164 + 95 = 259.

Players with representation for their national teams have played an average of 259 matches in their career. The difference between

Table 3.3 Total number of matches played by national team representation. Linear regression

Independent variable	*b*
National team representation (no = 0; yes = 1)	95
Constant	164
R^2	0.11
N	310

these predictions, as we already know, is our regression coefficient: 95 matches. I mentioned earlier that the constant was the point where the regression line crossed the y-axis. If you move straight down from this point you will land at, you guessed it, $x = 0$.

When x has only two values, 0 or 1, a scatterplot is no longer a very intuitive device for showing regression results. We are then left with the table solution presented in Table 3.3. We notice in passing that the national team representation dummy explains 11 percent of the variation in the number of matches played variable.

We have now seen that linear regression can be used to handle both quantitative and categorical independent variables or x-es. In fact, the only requisite for linear regression to work properly is that the dependent variable, y, is quantitative or nearly so. This versatility is what makes regression such a flexible statistical technique and a popular choice. Regression is also handy for cases in which several independent variables or x-es affect y at the same time, something that Chapter 5 digs much deeper into. Other statistical techniques might also be used for this purpose, such as ANOVA (analysis of variance) or ANCOVA (analysis of covariance). But since linear regression does everything that ANOVA/ANCOVA can do and more, I have decided to save the ANOVA approach for a special topics section at the end of this chapter.

CASE STUDY 3: THE PRICE, QUALITY RATING, AND ALCOHOL CONTENT OF BEERS, CONT.

You might recall from Chapter 2 that our beers were brewed in two countries: Sweden or the USA. (And if you did not, well, now you do.) Our research question is to examine whether there is an association between the country where a beer is produced and its alcohol content. The Swedish beers are coded 0, and the US beers are coded 1. My statistics program finds the regression equation to be:

Alcohol content = 6.88 + 1.30 × production country.

Four conclusions emerge. First, since 1.30 is much more than 0.00, we have an association between the variables. Second, US beers have an alcohol content that is 1.30 percentage points higher than that of Swedish beers on average. Third, Swedish beers, again on average, have an alcohol content of 6.88 (as per the constant). Fourth and finally, the average alcohol content of US beers is 8.18: 6.88 + 1.30 = 8.18. Pretty neat, right?

CASE STUDY 4: THE WELL-BEING OF NORWEGIANS, CONT.

Our y is the 11-point subjective well-being variable measured by the question, "How satisfied are you with your life?" I continue to treat this variable as quantitative, although it is ordinal in the strict sense. Our x is a dummy variable indicating the presence of any long-lasting illnesses or health problems: no = 0; yes = 1. Our research question concerns finding out about any possible association between these two variables. Table 3.4 displays the regression results. On the 11-point scale, respondents with long-lasting illnesses or health problems report an average of 0.81 points *lower* subjective well-being than respondents without such illness or health problems. We find an association between the two variables, much as to be expected.

Table 3.4 Subjective well-being by the presence of long-lasting illnesses or health problems. Linear regression

Independent variable	b
Long-lasting illnesses or health problems (no = 0; yes = 1)	−0.81
Constant	8.42
R^2	0.06
N	6,539

SOME CONSIDERATIONS ON R²

R-squared, or R^2, measures how much of the *variance* in the dependent variable, y, being explained by the independent variable, x. In other words, it is the variance and not the variation that is of concern. Yet this distinction is of minor importance. The more critical issue concerns the general role of R^2 in regression-based research. Some argue that it plays, or should play, a minor role. Others view a regression with an R^2 of 15 percent or less as pretty much useless. Whatever the stance, we should never refer to an R^2 of, say, 30 percent as good or bad in and on itself. R^2 should always, if at all, be judged in comparison to some benchmark, typically to be found in prior research.

WHEN BOTH THE INDEPENDENT VARIABLE, *X*, AND THE DEPENDENT VARIABLE, *Y*, ARE CATEGORICAL VARIABLES

Regression analysis or some extension of it is typically used whenever quantitative variables are in the mix. But when that is not the case, which often occurs in the social and behavioral sciences, we often employ other statistical techniques. We return to our football player data once more for an example.

We have already seen that some of the players have represented their national teams, while others have not. And I can be more exact since I know these percentages to be 19 percent (represented) and 81 percent (not represented). This is a nominal variable, or dummy. Another dummy variable in the football data is the nationality of the players: Norwegian or foreign. The present research question is to find out whether these nominal variables or dummies are associated. To do so, we use a statistical technique called cross-tabulation. The result of a cross-tabulation is a cross-table. (Some call it a contingency table, but I'll stick with cross-table.) The results are presented in Table 3.5.

The total column on the right-hand side shows what we already knew: 19 percent of the players have represented their national team. The new information stems from the four numbers in the cells to the left of the total column (clockwise): 86, 70, 30, and 14. Among the foreign players, 30 percent have represented national teams, while the similar number for the Norwegian players is 14 percent. This difference is 16 percentage points ($30 - 14 = 16$). So, a player's nationality seems to have an impact on the chances of representing his national team. Or as we have learned by now: the variables seem to be associated. Generally, we have that the larger the difference in percent, the stronger the association. (Note that the percentage difference is also 16 for the no-category of national team representation. This follows with necessity whenever a table has only four cells.)

The two variables in Table 3.5 are both nominal, and each of them has two categories. We thus call it a 2 × 2 cross-table. But cross-tabulations are not restricted to just the 2 × 2 cases or to categorical variables only. They can in fact be applied to any type of variable, provided that the number of categories is reasonably small, like four or five. Why four or five? Well, any cross-table with more than about 20 cells can get very tricky to interpret.

The research question driving Table 3.6 is whether there is an association between player nationality and position on the pitch. None of the percentage differences are larger than 6 percentage points (for the strikers). The variables appear not to be associated.

Table 3.5 National team representation by nationality. Cross-tabulation. Percentages

| National team representation | Nationality | | |
	Norwegian	Foreign	Total
No	86	70	81
Yes	14	30	19
Total	100 (214)	100 (96)	100 (310)

Note. Numbers in parentheses are actual frequencies (i.e., number of units).

Table 3.6 Player position by nationality. Cross-tabulation. Percentages

| Player position | Nationality | | |
	Norwegian	Foreign	Total
Defender	38	33	36
Midfielder	29	28	29
Winger	19	19	19
Striker	14	20	16
Total	100 (214)	100 (96)	100 (310)

Note. Numbers in parentheses are actual frequencies (i.e., number of units).

The variables in Tables 3.5 and 3.6 are nominal. In contrast, the goal-scoring variable in Table 3.7, a quantitative variable at the outset, has been *recoded* into an ordinal variable with three categories. Several percentage differences must now be compared for the scoring categories, but we instantly notice the pattern: defenders and midfielders are overrepresented among those who do not score goals. Conversely, wingers and strikers (and especially the latter) are more typical among those who score more than four goals. We find a clear association between the variables, as to be expected.

Cross-tables might also be presented as graphs, as Figure 3.5 shows.

Table 3.7 Goal-scoring by player position. Cross-tabulation. Percentages

Goals scored	Player position				
	Defender	Midfielder	Winger	Striker	Total
0	47	28	17	12	30
1–3	46	54	54	29	47
4–2	7	18	29	59	23
Total	100 (113)	100 (89)	100 (59)	100 (49)	100 (310)

Note. Numbers in parentheses are actual frequencies (i.e., number of units).

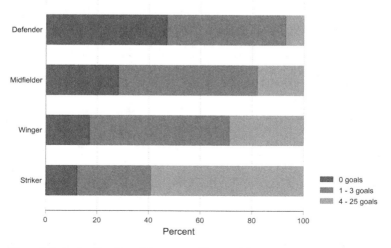

Figure 3.5 A visualization of the cross-table in Table 3.7

CASE STUDY 4: THE WELL-BEING OF NORWEGIANS, CONT.

We know that some proportion of the Norwegian population reports having long-lasting illnesses or health problems; cf. Table 3.4. To be specific, that proportion is 38 percent (as shown in Table 3.8). Our present research question is to find out about any possible association between this health-problem dummy and the biological sex of the respondent. The cross-table in Table 3.8 explores this idea. It turns out that females report having long-lasting illnesses or health problems more frequently than males, with the difference being 8 percentage points. In other words, we find a smallish association between the two dummy variables.

We have now covered the basics on how to associate two variables, typically called bivariate data analysis in the lingo: correlation, regression, and cross-tabulation. I close this chapter with some "special" topics.

Table 3.8 Long-lasting illnesses or health problems by sex. Cross-tabulation. Percentages

| Long-lasting illnesses or health problems | Sex | | |
	Male	Female	Total
No	66	58	62
Yes	34	42	38
Total	100 (3,330)	100 (3,258)	100 (6,550)

Note. Numbers in parentheses are actual frequencies (i.e., number of units).

SPECIAL TOPIC 1: REGRESSION WITH A DUMMY X VERSUS ANOVA (ANALYSIS OF VARIANCE)

Table 3.3 showed that football players with no representation for their national teams had played an average of 164 matches in their career, as per the constant. (Go check if you do not remember!) And since the regression coefficient was 95 matches, players with representation for their national teams had played an average of 259 matches (164 + 95 = 259). In other words, regression calculates the average for subgroup A in the data (as defined by the constant) and the difference between this A-group average and the B-group average.

Table 3.9 Total number of matches played by national team representation. ANOVA. N = 310

	Mean
National team representation	
No	164
Yes	259

This difference *is* the regression coefficient. ANOVA, in contrast, calculates the two averages directly, as you can see in Table 3.9. We must then ourselves calculate the difference between the two group averages – that is, the regression coefficient – by subtracting the smaller mean from the larger one (259 − 164 = 95).

In practice, as I mentioned earlier, regression with a dummy *x* and ANOVA boil down to the same. For reasons we get back to in Chapter 5, however, the regression approach offers more flexibility than the ANOVA approach. We are therefore going to set aside ANOVA from now on (mostly) but see the further reading section.

SPECIAL TOPIC 2: NON-LINEAR (REGRESSION) ASSOCIATIONS

Our regression lines have so far all been linear. This is a simplification made by the analyst: me, in this case. In other words, when we tell our statistics program to do a linear regression, we are essentially *forcing* the *x*–*y* association to be summarized as a straight line regardless of what that association looks like in real life. Sometimes we know that the *x*–*y* association in question is non-linear, though. In these cases, we should adjust our regression-thinking and perform some kind of non-linear regression. We return to our data on Norwegians' well-being for an application.

Figure 3.6 is a scatterplot showing the association between yearly income and age for 6,547 Norwegians between 18 and 70 years of age.

Before we dive into the technicalities of non-linear regression, one point is worth mentioning about Figure 3.6. Whenever we analyze more than, say, 1,000 units in statistics, it becomes challenging to discern any patterns in the data just by looking at a scatterplot. This has important implications for the analysis of "big data," where

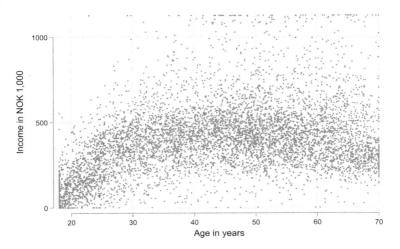

Figure 3.6 Scatterplot of yearly income and age among Norwegians

we are typically working with 100,000s or millions of units. In short, scatterplots often get us nowhere when it comes to analyzing big or even moderately big data.

With 6,547 respondents being present in Figure 3.6, it is expectedly tough to discern any pattern in the data. By upon closer inspection, we nevertheless notice that the data points are not spread out in a random fashion. No, most of them are tightly clustered in the middle and toward the lower left of the plot. We may ask a statistics program for help in this regard, by providing us with the trend line the data points themselves suggest as the best overall summary of the association between the two variables.[8] Figure 3.7 shows us this *data-driven* trend line.

The take-home message of Figure 3.7 is that the data suggest a *non-linear* association between age and income. Income tends to increase with age, but only up to a certain age point. (Technically correct, we have that income tends to peak among middle aged people.) This inflection or tipping point is around the age of 50. Beyond that, income tends to decrease with age on average.

Having established that age and income are non-linearly associated, it makes much sense to adjust our regression line to reflect this. Fortunately, this is child's play for any statistics program worth

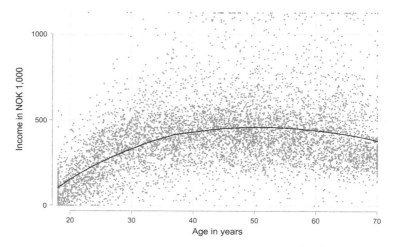

Figure 3.7 Scatterplot of yearly income and age among Norwegians, with data-driven trend line

its salt. Figure 3.8 overlays the linear and non-linear regression lines on the scatterplot. As you might expect, the linear regression assumes that income increases indefinitely with age, whereas the non-linear regression suggests that income starts to decline after about 50 years of age. But this raises an important question: how can we be sure that the non-linear regression provides a better description of the real-world association between age and income than the linear regression? Well, we cannot be 100 percent certain, but R^2 provides some guidance. While the linear regression in Figure 3.8 has an R^2 of 10.5 percent, the non-linear regression has an R^2 of 23.1 percent. In this way, we can use R^2 as a benchmark for comparing the fit of the two regression models. And according to this criterion, the non-linear regression model has a closer fit to the data points than the linear model. (It also helps a lot that any non-linear pattern makes some kind of theoretical sense!)

We call the non-linear association depicted in Figure 3.7 an inverted U-pattern. The opposite, a U-pattern, implies a regression line that first decreases and then increases. As a practical matter, the inverted U-bend is probably most common in in the behavioral and social sciences.[9]

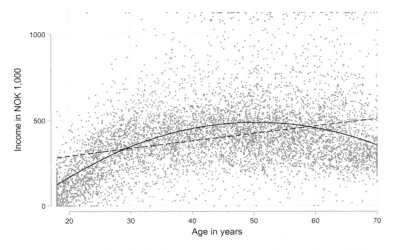

Figure 3.8 Scatterplot of yearly income and age among Norwegians, with linear regression line (dashed) and non-linear regression line (solid)

SPECIAL TOPIC 3: ORDINAL DEPENDENT VARIABLES

Ordinal dependent variables are sometimes straightforward to analyze – and sometimes not. When the ordinal y has many categories, like subjective well-being in Table 3.4, matters are often simple: we treat it as quantitative. End of story. Matters become less clear-cut when y has only a few ordinal categories. We return to our wine club data from Chapter 2. The dependent variable, y, is the Likert-statement, "I often discuss wine with my family, friends, and colleagues." The answer categories are totally disagree, disagree, neither disagree nor agree, agree, or totally agree, with codings from 0 (totally disagree) to 4 (totally agree). The independent variable, x, is the biological sex of the wine club member, coded 0 for females and 1 for males. As before, our research question asks if these variables are associated. The cross-table in Table 3.10 answers this question.

When looking at the totally-agree answers, we see that male members report this more often than female members. The percentages are 41 (male) and 24 (female), making the sex difference 17 percentage points ($41 - 24 = 17$). For the remaining categories, however, female members are overrepresented. It appears as if the two variables are somewhat associated.

Table 3.10 Wine statement by sex. Cross-tabulation. Percentages

Wine statement[a]	Sex		
	Female	Male	Total
Totally disagree	2	0	1
Disagree	8	6	7
Neither/nor	19	14	16
Agree	48	38	42
Totally agree	24	41	34
Total	100 (189)	100 (279)	100 (468)

Note. Numbers in parentheses are actual frequencies (i.e., number of units).

[a] The statement reads, "I often discuss wine with my family, friends, and colleagues."

In situations where our y has five ordinal categories, like in this example, we could consider treating it as a quantitative variable: a scale ranging from 0 (totally disagree) to 4 (totally agree). The wine statement variable has a mean score of 3.02 on this coarse scale (not shown). If we choose to take this approach, we may apply linear regression in the normal manner, as in:

Answer to wine statement = a + b × biological sex.

My statistics program tells me that the relevant numbers become:

Answer to wine statement = 2.85 + 0.28 × biological sex.

Since biological sex is coded 1 for males and 0 for females, the on average-interpretation is that male wine club members score 0.28-points *higher* on the wine statement scale than female members. So, there seems to be an association between the two variables, which aligns well with what we already know from Table 3.10. Male members tend to (totally) agree with the statement more often than female members do.

Sometimes it makes good sense to treat a five-category ordinal y-variable as a quantitative variable, like we just did. In others, it might make much less sense. Unfortunately, there are no hard-and-fast rules about when it is ok to do this and when it is not. That said, some statistics textbooks are entirely devoted to ordinal variables; cf. the further reading section.

KEY LEARNING POINTS

The key learning points in this chapter were:

- A correlation, typically expressed in a scatterplot, shows the (possibly linear) association between two quantitative variables.
- The strength of a correlation is measured by the correlation coefficient. The larger the correlation coefficient, the tighter the data points are clustered around a linear (straight) line.
- The correlation coefficient ranges from perfectly negative (−1) via 0 (no linear correlation) and to perfectly positive (+1).
- Regression analysis might be thought of as a more sophisticated type of correlation.
- Regression analysis is (at the outset) concerned with finding the steepness of the regression line associating a quantitative independent variable, x, and a quantitative dependent variable, y.
- The steepness of the regression line is measured by the regression coefficient (aka slope).
- The technical interpretation of the regression coefficient (or slope) is the change in y resulting from a one-unit increase in x.
- The point where the regression line crosses the y-axis is called the constant (aka intercept).
- R^2 measures how much of the variation (variance, to be precise) in y that is explained by variation in x.
- Regression can also handle categorical x-variables.
- We call a nominal variable with two categories a dummy variable or dummy.
- When both x and y are categorical variables, we typically associate them by means of a cross-tabulation.
- An association between a quantitative y and a categorical x might also be examined by means of ANOVA.
- Regression analysis can be extended to allow for non-linear associations between x and y.
- When an ordinal y has many values (more than five or six, say), we often treat it as a "partially" quantitative variable and use regression or ANOVA.

NOTES

1   See Agresti (2018). The correlation coefficient in the main text is known as the Pearson correlation coefficient or r. There are other types of correlation coefficients, but Pearson's version is by far the dominant one in applied statistical analysis in the social and behavioral sciences.

2   Or more correctly, since we are comparing players at the same point in time, that a 26-year-old player, on average, has played 23 more matches than a 25-year-old player.

3   Another name for the constant is the intercept.

4   In a bivariate regression (aka a regression with one x-variable), R^2 or R-squared is, yes, the *square* of the Pearson correlation coefficient (r).

5   That said, since none of the football players in the data are zero years of age (obviously!), this would-be start of the regression line is a figment of imagination.

6   Of course, akin to in endnote 4, the possibility of zero diners taking part in a meal is also a figment of imagination. Or is it?

7   Just to be clear. We call *any* variable – independent or dependent – with two categories a dummy variable or a dummy.

8   The statistical technique yielding the non-linear line (in this case) is called a scatterplot smoother. See the further reading section.

9   Both patterns show up under the heading of polynomial regression in many textbooks; see Chapter 8 and the further reading section.

FURTHER READING

In addition to the books already mentioned in the further reading section, I recommend Agresti (2018) and Thrane (2020, 2022) as follow-ups to this chapter. Agresti (2010) is explicitly about the analysis of ordinal variables.

APPENDIX: A SHORT PRIMER ON BIVARIATE LINEAR REGRESSION ANALYSIS

Most textbooks present the bivariate regression model in a more technical way than the laid-back approach I have taken in this chapter. First, we denote the constant or a (aka the intercept) as b_0. Second, we denote the regression coefficient or slope as b_1. Third, we leave out the multiplication sign between b_1 and x because it is implied. And finally, the bivariate regression model includes a so-called error term, e, which accounts for random variation and all other x-variables' effects on y. So, we write the general bivariate regression model in our data as:

$$y = b_0 + b_1 x + e.$$

But since we assume that the influence of e on y is zero on average, we skip it in the daily doings of regression. (In practice, this assumption needs testing, but that is technical stuff we set aside for chapter 8.) So, the bivariate regression model we ask our statistics program to estimate for our data is simply:

$$y = b_0 + b_1 x.$$

Figure 3.A.1 schematically shows the regression line based on the above equation. The interpretation of the regression coefficient, b_1, is the change in y when x increases by one unit. The constant, b_0, is where the regression line starts on the y-axis, namely for $x = 0$. All statistics programs estimate the value of b_0 and b_1 based on the units' values for x and y in the data. The estimation method is known as the *method of least squares*. The crux of this procedure is to find the line that minimizes the sum of the distances from the data points to the regression line. That is why linear regression also is known as OLS (Ordinary Least Squares) regression.

Every statistics textbook will walk you through the calculations needed to perform this procedure on a small data set, and I encourage you to check out the further reading section for details. The output from statistics programs (like Stata, R, SPSS, and so on) generally look very similar. Stata-output 3.1 provides an example of such an output for the football regression in Table 3.1.

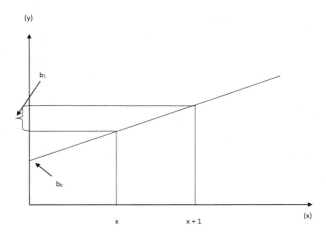

Figure 3.A.1 The regression line, b_0 (the constant), and b_1 (the regression coefficient)

Stata–output 3.1 Results in Stata yielding Table 3.1.

Source	SS	df	MS	Number of obs	=	310
				F(1, 308)	=	1087.46
Model	2873797.7	1	2873797.7	Prob > F	=	0.0000
Residual	813942.682	308	2642.67105	R-squared	=	0.7793
				Adj R-squared	=	0.7786
Total	3687740.39	309	11934.4349	Root MSE	=	51.407

matches	Coefficient	Std. err.	t	P>|t|	[95% conf. interval]	
age	22.90249	.6945062	32.98	0.000	21.53591	24.26907
_cons	-403.2413	17.97992	-22.43	0.000	-438.6203	-367.8623

The regression coefficient/b_1 for the age of player variable (age) is 22.90, the constant/b_0 is -403.24 (_cons), and R^2 (R-squared) is almost 0.78 or 78 percent. The analysis is based on 310 units (obs). We return to some of the other numbers in this output in Chapter 4.

INFERENTIAL STATISTICAL ANALYSIS

CHAPTER OVERVIEW

DOI: 10.4324/9781032640808-4

INTRODUCTION

In Chapters 2 and 3, we explored descriptive and associational research questions in terms of what occurred in our data. Now, it is time to take a step further and tackle inferential questions. Inferential questions are about making correct inferences or generalizations from our data to other people, situations, or settings. But let me first give you a heads up. Inferential statistics is a notch tougher to grasp than the statistical concepts we have covered so far in this book. That is why I promise to stick to the KISS-principle in this chapter: Keep It Sensibly Simple!

POPULATIONS, SAMPLES, AND RANDOM SAMPLING

So far, we have only briefly touched on two key concepts in inferential statistics: *population* and *sample*. A population refers to all the units sharing a particular feature, like all the football players in Premier League or all the citizens of Germany aged between 18 and 70 years. But populations are not limited to people; all the ice creams sold in Denmark in 2023 also qualify as a population. The same goes for all traffic accidents in Italy in January 2024.

Populations are what interests us as analysts in research settings. Historically, however, modern-day statistical analysis has largely carried out calculations on samples rather than populations. A sample, by definition, is some subset of units from a larger population. Why, then, has the analysis of samples been the norm in research? In many ways, this has been a choice of necessity since directly studying populations was nearly impossible or too time-consuming or resource-intensive. Plus, statisticians discovered long ago that it worked just fine to examine a (small) sample to get information about the complete (large) population from which the sample was drawn. Or more precisely, this worked fine if the sample in question was *representative* of the population. But this raises the question of how to get a representative sample from a larger population? The answer is to do *random sampling*.

A lottery is an apt metaphor for a random sampling process. In Norway, the state-run lottery works like this. First, 34 lottery balls, each numbered from 1 to 34, are loaded into an urn or box. Second, the box starts to spin, and the 34 balls get mixed around. Third, a mechanical device randomly selects one of the 34 balls.

The procedure then starts all over again: the spin-and-mix routine resulting in a selection of a second ball from the 33 remaining balls, and so on until five balls have been selected in total. The numbers on these five balls are the winning numbers for the main prize. Now for a large-scale thought experiment against this background.

Picture a box filled with 750,000 balls, each numbered from 1 to 750,000. Now, imagine selecting 300 balls from this box using the procedure as I just described above. The probability of selecting, say, ball number 25,634 in the first selection is 1/750,000. Next, the probability of selecting, say, ball number 589,187 in the second selection is 1/749,999. For the third ball and number, the probability becomes 1/749,998, and so on for the 297 remaining balls. These lotteries – the actual version and our large-scale thought version – are similar in principle. But there is a subtle difference. In the real lottery, the first ball has a selection probability of 1/34, while the fifth ball's selection probability is 1/30. So, the last ball has a higher selection probability than the first. And although this difference might seem small, it is not entirely negligible. In our thought version lottery, in contrast, the difference in selection probability between the first and the last ball is miniscule: 1/750,000 versus 1/749,700. And this, without going into details, makes all the difference in the world.

Our lottery scenarios may be thought of as examples of random sampling. Yet only the large-scale thought version satisfies the most stringent requirement of random sampling: that every unit in the population has a *known and equal* chance of being selected into the sample. In other words, for all practical purposes, 1/750,000 is effectively equal to 1/749,700. (For the record, this is known as sampling without replacement. For sampling with replacement, we put the selected ball back into the box before each new draw. But let's not go there.)

FROM PRECISE SAMPLE FINDINGS TO APPROXIMATE POPULATION KNOWLEDGE

Random sampling ensures that a sample gets representative of the larger population from which it is drawn, at least most of the time. This idea really is quite amazing; by studying just a small fraction of a population, we learn about the whole population! But there is a catch. The results for our random sample might differ from the actual results in the unknown population due to random differences between the sample and the population. This is why we always must answer one question when analyzing a random sample: could random chance differences between the unknown population and our known sample in any way account for our sample findings? If the answer is yes, we cannot confidently claim that what we find in our sample applies to the population. But if the answer is no, we maintain that our sample findings are also population findings. When a sample result is considered to reflect a population result in this way, we say that it is "statistically significant." This chapter will get us there ... We start by returning to our pizza restaurant data, which were chosen for this book because they were generated in a way akin to the random sampling procedures I just described.[1] Hold on tight!

CASE STUDY 1: THE TYPICAL QUANTITATIVE CHARACTERISTICS OF PIZZA RESTAURANT MEALS, CONT.

The pizza restaurant data concern the characteristics of 300 meals, as outlined in Tables 2.4 and 2.5. The way I described the collection of these data in Chapter 2 was bogus, though. My apologies! The truth is, I have a data set of 750,000 pizza restaurant meals on my computer. This data set, which covers all the meals bought in a Norwegian pizza restaurant chain over a year, is a population. From this population, I used a random number generator (mimicking a lottery) to randomly select the 300 meals in the sample. So, these data are a random sample from a large population. However, it is not customary to have access to a sample *and* the population from which this sample is drawn. On the contrary, we usually have access to samples only. (With the advent of "big data" and administrative record data, population data have become more common of late, though.) Yet having access to both types of data can be a useful teaching tool for the purpose of showing the workings of inferential statistics. Because now we can compare the sample findings with the population findings. Let's begin with the variable total bill for the meal. Table 4.1 shows the most important descriptive results for this variable. In addition, Figure 4.1 depicts this variable's distribution and compares it with the normal distribution.

Table 4.1 Descriptive statistics for total bill. N = 300

	Mean	*SD*	*Min*	*Max*
Total bill for meal	522.677	318.672	105	2,298

Note. Total bill is in Norwegian Krone (NOK). NOK 100 has traditionally been the equivalent of roughly €10 or $11.

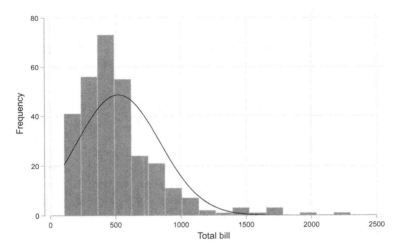

Figure 4.1 Histogram of total bill for meal in Norwegian Krone, with normal distribution superimposed

The average total bill in the sample is NOK 523, and the bill variable's distribution is characterized by a right skew: a few costly meals pull the mean upward and away from the median of NOK 455 (not shown). But let's set the median aside for now and concentrate on the mean. What is the mean of the total bill variable in the unknown population? Well, the short answer is that we usually do not know this. The longer and more helpful answer is that we may estimate this unknown mean based on information from the sample only – at least approximately. We need three numbers to do this: the mean, the standard deviation (SD), and the sample size. Before we dive into that, though, we should introduce a new concept: *the standard error* or SE.

The SE resembles the SD we saw in Chapter 2. The SD measures the magnitude of a variable's variation: how close or far the units tend to be located from the sample mean. Like the SD, the SE is also a measure of variation. But unlike the SD, which relates to the distribution of a real-life variable, the SE does no such thing. No, the SE refers to the variation in something known as the *sampling distribution*. What, then, is a sampling distribution? Here we go.

I told my statistics program to draw one random sample of 300 meals from my population of 750,000 meals. For this sample, as we saw in Table 4.1, the mean of the total bill variable was NOK 523. Yet for the sake of this book, I also drew 499 more samples in exactly the same manner. Then, for each of these samples, I calculated and recorded the mean of the total bill variable. The first six of these means, as well as the last one (mean number 500), is shown in Table 4.2.

You can now think of Table 4.2 as a new data set with 500 units and one variable: the variable "Total bill: mean." The histogram for this mean-of-means variable is shown in Figure 4.2.

The distribution shown in Figure 4.2 is the *sampling distribution* of the total bill variable. Strictly speaking, a sampling distribution is the result of an indefinite and unknown repeated sampling process, whereas I stopped at 500 random draws for practical reasons. Since we can never know what the actual sampling distribution looks like, I should above probably have written "sampling distribution" or *estimated* sampling distribution. But that seems excessive in this teaching context. For our purposes, we simply assume that my estimated sampling distribution is the actual sampling distribution.

Table 4.2 Results of repeated sampling for the restaurant meal data

Sample number	Total bill: mean
Sample 1	523
Sample 2	535
Sample 3	513
Sample 4	526
Sample 5	507
Sample 6	515
Sample ...	...
Sample ...	...
Sample 500	532

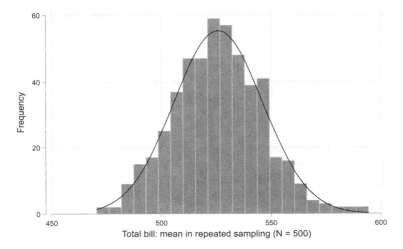

Figure 4.2 Histogram of "Total bill: mean" in repeated sampling, with normal
distribution superimposed

We observe a peculiar result when comparing Figures 4.1 and
4.2. The distribution of the total bill variable in our sample is not at
all normally distributed. Yet the bill variable's sampling distribution
is very much normally distributed. This phenomenon is known as
the Central Limit Theorem (CLT) in statistics, and it is handy for a
bunch of statistical applications (see the appendix to this chapter and
the further reading section).

Like all distributions, the sampling distribution is characterized
by central tendency and variation. The mean of this distribution is
known as the *sampling mean*, while the variation of this distribution is *not* known as the sampling SD (as it perhaps should). No,
it is known as the SE and measures the variation in a variable's
sampling distribution. (Both the sampling mean and the SE are
unknown in practice because we do not observe the sampling
distribution.) Long story short: we use our sample knowledge to
estimate the SE for the unknown sampling distribution. The formula to get this SE is:

$$\frac{s}{\sqrt{n}},$$

where s is the SD for the total bill variable in our sample, and n is the number of meals (units) in our sample.[2] From Table 3.1, we calculate that our SE becomes:

$$\frac{318.672}{\sqrt{300}} = 18.399 \approx 18.4.$$

After this strenuous voyage, we have what we need to construct a 95 percent confidence interval or CI for the total bill variable. The premise is that any normally distributed variable (akin to the sampling distribution depicted in Figure 4.2) is characterized by that 95 percent of its units fall within the interval: mean $\pm$ 1.96 $\times$ standard deviations or SDs.[3] So, to get a 95 percent CI, we "simply" replace this with:

95 percent CI for a mean = sample mean $\pm$ 1.96 $\times$ SEs.

The 95 percent CI for the total bill variable then becomes:

$$522.7 \pm 1.96 \times 18.4 = 522.7 \pm 36.1 = [486.6, 558.8].$$

Here is the *rough* interpretation of this CI: given a sample mean of NOK 523, we are 95 percent confident that the population mean falls within the range of NOK 487–559.[4] So, the cost of a typical pizza restaurant meal in the population is most likely somewhere between NOK 490 and NOK 560.

We have now managed to draw a conclusion about the unknown population using only sample information, just like I promised we could do. Even so, we paid a price. While the results for our sample are clear-cut and precise, the results for our population are less clear-cut and approximate. This was the first leg of going from precise sample results to more approximate population results. But since we in the present case also know the true value of the population mean, we can compare our results. Drum roll, please … The population mean is NOK 525. We nailed it!

We have just calculated a 95 percent CI for a sample mean. Logically, there must also be a similar CI for the *difference* between two such means. Moreover, all the statistical association measures we have seen so far (correlation coefficient, regression coefficient, percentage difference) have similar 95 percent CIs. So, we can calculate all CIs using the setup just described if we are dealing with a so-called large sample. In practice, this implies a sample containing more than 120 units. We have:

95 percent CI for *anything* = sample *anything* ± 1.96 × SEs.

In a school exam, the challenge is to remember the various formulas for calculating the SE in this or that context. But since we are in the business of doing statistical analysis rather than passing exams, we can leave these calculations to our statistics program. (As always, you find the formulas in any textbooks on statistics or with a quick search on Google. Or see the further reading section.)

THE 95 PERCENT CI FOR A DIFFERENCE IN TWO MEANS

Table 2.5 indicated that 31 percent of the pizza restaurant meals included the consumption of alcohol, implying that 69 percent did not. The mean of the total bill variable among the meals accompanied by alcohol is NOK 578 (n = 94). The similar mean for the meals not accompanied by alcohol is NOK 497 (n = 206). The difference between these sample means is NOK 81 (578 − 497 = 81). It seems as if alcohol with the meal entails a higher total bill on average. Yet this NOK 81 mean difference applies only to our sample. What is this difference in the population? We do not know. But we can estimate a 95 percent CI that probably encompasses this difference. We use the "formula":

95 percent CI for a difference between two means = sample difference between two means ± 1.96 × SEs.

We have the sample difference, NOK 81, and our statistics program finds the SE for us.[5] It is 39. The 95 percent CI becomes:

81 ± 1.96 × 39 ﹔81 ± 76.4 = [4.6, 157.4].

Given a sample mean difference of NOK 81, we are 95 percent confident that the mean difference in the population falls within the interval from NOK 5 to NOK 157. This interval does *not* contain zero, which would suggest that meals with and without alcohol have the same total bill on average. We can therefore infer that, on average, meals with alcohol entail a larger total bill than meals without alcohol in the population. The sample result appears to apply as a result for the population as well.

We calculate CIs for correlation coefficients and regression coefficients in the same manner as above: sample coefficient ± 1.96 × SEs. You can find the CI for the player age variable on the right-hand side of Stata-output 3.1, under [95% conf. interval]. If a CI does not contain zero, we claim that the coefficient − or in general: the statistical association − applies to the population. If a CI does include zero, however, we cannot confidently claim that the association exists in the population; it might just be a statistical fluke. This marks the second leg of going from precise sample results to approximate population results. Now for the third and final leg.

HYPOTHESIS TESTING AND SIGNIFICANCE LEVELS

In this section, I explicate the conventional way of conducting and interpreting a hypothesis test. (I'll look more closely at the criticism of this approach in Chapter 7.) A hypothesis test is the formal way of determining whether two variables are associated in a population based on the analysis of sample data. So, we should assume at the outset that the data we are analyzing are a random sample from a large population. The general setup is similar for the statistical techniques we have encountered so far: correlation, regression, analysis of variance (ANOVA), and cross-tabulation. But since regression is the work horse of statistical analysis, I initially demonstrate the general approach using a regression example.

Table 3.2 and Figure 3.3 showed an association between the total bill for the meal and the number of diners taking part in it − *in the sample*. The regression coefficient was 125. This coefficient also has a 95 percent CI, of course, but that is old news. The task at hand is to test whether these two variables are associated in the population. This kind of hypothesis testing always involves two hypotheses: the null hypothesis and the alternative hypothesis. The alternative hypothesis is what we believe in for the population based on prior research, common sense, or a hunch. In our example, this alternative hypothesis (H_1) is:

> H_1 There is an association between the number of diners and the total bill for the meal.

The null hypothesis, in contrast, reads:

> H_0 There is no association between the number of diners and the total bill for the meal.

In a way, the null hypothesis expresses the "opposite" of our (prior) beliefs. And perhaps contrary to intuition, we always test the null hypothesis; we test what we do not believe in against what the sample data show us. If the sample data show us something that does not align well with the null hypothesis, we reject it. This rejection of the null hypothesis indirectly supports the alternative hypothesis, namely what we believed in at the outset. Let's see how this works for our restaurant example.

The null hypothesis suggests no association between the number of diners and the total bill for the meal in the population. This translates into a regression coefficient of zero. (A regression coefficient of zero yields a horizontal regression line, indicating no association between x and y.) So, the null hypothesis suggests a regression coefficient of zero in the unknown population, whereas the sample regression coefficient is 125. Is this alignment? To answer this question, we put the formula for the CI on its head to get us an interval called the *acceptance region* for the null hypothesis. This "formula" is simply:

Acceptance region of H_0 = 0 ± 1.96 × SEs.

In essence, we are looking for the "confidence interval" of a regression coefficient we now assume is zero in the population. In our example, the statistics program calculates this regression coefficient's SE to be 9.61. The acceptance region then becomes:

$0 ± 1.96 × 9.61 \rightarrow 0 ± 18.84 = [-18.84, 18.84].$

Assuming the null hypothesis is true (i.e., there is a regression coefficient of zero in the population), the interval from NOK −19 to NOK 19 will, 95 percent of the time, contain the regression coefficient of zero if we draw many repeated samples of $n = 300$ and repeat the regression for each sample. Down here on earth, we say that our sample coefficient of NOK 125 falls outside the acceptance region of the null hypothesis. This means that what our sample data show us does not align with what the null hypothesis suggests. So, we reject the null hypothesis and get indirect support for the alternative hypothesis. In the lingo, we say that the association between the number of diners and the total bill for the meal is *statistically significant*. The association exists, so to speak, in the population.

Thankfully, we do not have to follow this roundabout route every time we test a hypothesis. At this stage, though, things become much simpler if we look at the output from a statistics program. Stata-output 4.1 (akin to Stata-output 3.1) presents the results for our restaurant data regression. You will find that other statistics programs produce outputs looking remarkably similar.

Stata-output 4.1 Total bill for meal by number of diners. Linear regression.

```
      Source |       SS           df       MS      Number of obs   =        300
-------------+----------------------------------   F(1, 298)       =     168.75
       Model |  10978003.3         1  10978003.3   Prob > F        =     0.0000
    Residual |  19386022.3       298  65053.7661   R-squared       =     0.3615
-------------+----------------------------------   Adj R-squared   =     0.3594
       Total |  30364025.6       299  101551.925   Root MSE        =     255.06

-------------------------------------------------------------------------------
     bill_tot | Coefficient  Std. err.      t    P>|t|     [95% conf. interval]
-------------+-----------------------------------------------------------------
    num_dine |   124.7867   9.606002    12.99   0.000     105.8825    143.6909
       _cons |    211.126   28.14302     7.50   0.000     155.7417    266.5102
-------------------------------------------------------------------------------
```

Let's look at the familiar stuff first. The regression coefficient for the number of diners variable (num_dine) is 124.79 or ≈ 125, the constant is 211.13 (_cons), and R^2 (R-squared) is 0.362 or 36.2 percent. The analysis is based on 300 units or meals (obs).

The regression coefficient's SE (Std. err.) is 9.61. The CI for the regression coefficient is roughly [106, 144] ([95% conf. interval]).

Now, let's dive into the new material. To determine whether a regression coefficient is statistically significant, we divide the regression coefficient by its SE: 124.79/9.61 = 12.99. This value is shown in the column t, which is short for *t*-value. The rule to remember for *t*-values is that if they are larger than 1.96 or smaller than −1.96 (as in being more negative), the sample regression coefficient falls *outside* the acceptance region of the null hypothesis (assuming a large sample). In such a case, we reject H_0 and get indirect support for H_1. In our example, because the *t*-value is 12.99 (12.99 > 1.96), we follow this course of action. We consider the regression coefficient to be statistically significant; there is an association between the two variables in the population.

When a *t*-value falls between −1.96 to 1.96 or roughly between −2 to 2, it falls *within* the acceptance region of H_0. In this case, we dare not reject H_0, and we must keep it. This means that the association is not statistically significant; we cannot claim that it exists in the population. Figure 4.3 illustrates H_0's acceptance region from $t = -1.96$ to $t = 1.96$, namely the interval between the areas in

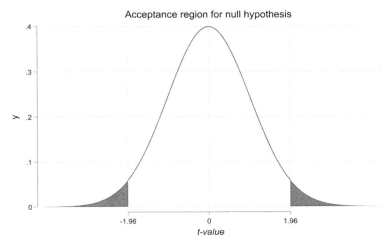

Figure 4.3 The acceptance region of the null hypothesis: the interval from $t = -1.96$ to $t = 1.96$

grey shading. In other words, and to rephrase, we reject the null hypothesis when the *t*-value falls on the right-hand side of 1.96 *or* on the left-hand side of −1.96.

The above explication implies that associations are either significant or not significant. This binary way of thinking, which we return to in Chapter 7, is generally not to be recommended. At present it is nevertheless more crucial to get a solid grip on two related concepts in inferential statistics: *p*-values and significance levels. This is coming up next.

You find the *p*-value on the right-hand side of the *t*-value in Stata–output 4.1, under the heading $P > |t|$. The *p* is short for *probability*. The *p*-value for the regression coefficient in question is 0.000, which means less than 0.0001 or less than 0.01 percent. We are talking about a miniscule probability. In our example, the *p*-value is the probability of finding a regression coefficient of NOK 125, or a larger one, *if* the true regression coefficient in the population is zero. Many people like to think of the *p*-value as the probability of random chance yielding the statistical association in the sample. It is not, at least not in the strict sense. (Sorry about that.)

The convention in statistics is that a *p*-value of $0.05 - 5$ percent − is the lowest form of confidence for which we reject a null hypothesis. This is known as the 5 percent significance level, and we denote it with one ⋆ (asterisk). When we reject a null hypothesis at $p = 0.05$, we accept a risk of doing something wrong up to five times out of 100 at the most, assuming the null hypothesis is true.[6] As it turns out (but let's not go there), a *p*-value of 0.05 exactly corresponds to a *t*-value of 1.96 or -1.96 in large samples. In this sense, *t*-values and *p*-values are like "opposite" mirror images: a large *t*-value implies a small *p*-value, and a large *p*-value implies a small *t*-value. Besides the 5 percent significance level, we also have the 1 percent level ($p < 0.01$ or ⋆⋆) and the 0.1 percent level ($p < 0.001$ or ⋆⋆⋆). Yet finding a sample regression coefficient or any other sample statistic with a lower significance level does not mean that the association is "more significant" as in being "more important." It just means that the probability of finding the association in the sample is even less likely assuming the null hypothesis is true for the population, all else being equal. This exposition of hypothesis testing and significance levels was the last leg of our journey through inferential statistics. Now it is time to move on to more practical topics. We start by revisiting

Norwegian's well-being based on the level-of-living survey from 2019. This survey pertained, as you now probably have guessed, to a random sample of the total population.

CASE STUDY 4: THE WELL-BEING OF NORWEGIANS, CONT.

Chapter 3 revealed an association between the presence of long-lasting illnesses or health problems and subjective well-being (cf. Table 3.4), as well as between the biological sex of the respondent and the presence of long-lasting illnesses or health problems (cf. Table 3.8). Yet both associations applied only to the sample. The research question now is whether these associations apply to the population as well. Tables 4.3 adds the necessary inferential statistics to Table 3.4.

As before and on average, people with long-lasting illnesses or health problems report 0.81 points *lower* subjective well-being (on the 11-point scale) than people with no such health problems. But this is sample information only. The new piece of information in the table is the SE: 0.041. By dividing the regression coefficient by its SE, we obtain the t-value of -19.8 ($-0.81/0.041 = -19.76$). This t-value is less than -1.96 (as in being more negative), corresponding to a p-value of less than 0.1 percent (★★★) as shown below the table.[7] Assuming a true null hypothesis for the population – that is, a regression coefficient of zero – it is highly unlikely to get a regression coefficient of -0.81 in a random sample from this population. So, we reject H_0 and get indirect support for an association between

Table 4.3 Subjective well-being by national presence of long-lasting illnesses or health problems. Linear regression

Independent variable	b
Long-lasting illnesses or health problems (no = 0; yes = 1)	-0.81★★★ (0.041)
Constant	8.42
R^2	0.06
N	6,539

Note. Standard errors are in parentheses.

★ $p < 0.05$; ★★ $p < 0.01$; ★★★ $p < 0.001$ (two-tailed tests).

the two variables in the population, as per H_1. The association is statistically significant at the 0.1 percent level. Table 4.3 also provides the information we need to construct the 95 percent CI for the regression coefficient: $-0.81 \pm 1.96 \times 0.041$. This interval is roughly $[-0.89, -0.73]$.

When doing regression analyses, we use a *t*-test to determine if there is an association between *x* and *y* in the population. When doing a cross-tabulation, in contrast, we perform something known as a *chi-square* test. Table 4.4 adds the necessary inferential statistics to complement Table 3.8.

Women report having long-lasting illnesses or health problems more often than men: 42 percent versus 34 percent. This sample difference is 8 percentage points. The intuition behind the chi-square test is straightforward: the null hypothesis for the population proposes that females and males report having long-lasting "troubles" to the same extent, suggesting no association between the variables. If that were true, and if our sample accurately represents the population, 38 percent of the females and 38 percent of the males *would* report of long-lasting troubles as per the total column on the right. But the actual percentages are 42 and 34, respectively. In other words, there is a discrepancy between what H_0 suggests (38 and 38) and what the sample results show us (42 and 34). The *p*-value is the probability of observing this 8-percentage points difference, or a larger one, if the true difference in the population is zero. The *p*-value in the note to the table tells us that this probability is very low indeed. Therefore, we reject H_0 and consider the association to be statistically significant at the 0.1 percent level. The association applies to the population.

Table 4.4 Long-lasting illnesses or health problems by sex. Cross-tabulation. Percentages

Long-lasting illnesses or health problems	Sex		
	Male	*Female*	*Total*
No	66	58	62
Yes	34	42	38
Total	100 (3,308)	100 (3,242)	100 (6,550)

Note. Numbers in parentheses are actual frequencies. Pearson chi-square $(1, n = 6,550) = 45.0, p < 0.001$.

A small sample caution. Before wrapping up this chapter, let me emphasize that all its content has assumed that the sample under examination is randomly selected from a large population and could be referred to as "large" itself, meaning more than 120 units or so. For samples smaller than this, we need *t*-values to be somewhat larger than 1.96 (or smaller than −1.96, as in being more negative) before we reject H_0 at the 5 percent level. For example, in a sample of about 30 units, this *t*-value is 2.042 (or −2.042). The same logic applies to chi-square values; see the further reading section for more details.

We have now taken a quick glance under the hood of inferential statistics. I close this chapter with some "special" topics. But first, let's get one thing right out of the way. You will often hear the phrase "*x* has a statistically significant effect on *y*." This does not mean − and will never mean! − that *x* has a large or important effect on *y* in any substantive sense. I have more to say on the use and misuse of significance testing in Chapter 7.

SPECIAL TOPIC 1: THE MARGIN OF ERROR, THE SAMPLE SIZE, AND THE PRECISION OF THE 95 PERCENT CI

Early on in this chapter, we saw that the sample mean of the total bill variable was 522.7. We also saw that this mean's 95 percent CI was [486.6, 558.8]. This CI, in turn, came from the calculation:

522.7 ± 1.96 × SEs,

where the SE was 18.4. The latter part of this expression, 1.96 × SEs, is known as the *margin of error*: approximately 36 in this case (1.96 × 18.4). Everything we calculate for a sample − means, differences between means, proportions, differences between proportions, regression coefficients − has a margin of error. This margin of error is generally given by the expression 1.96 SEs for large samples. (The multiplication symbol, ×, is redundant.)

We also noted earlier that the sample size was in the denominator when calculating the SE.[8] For this reason, the SE becomes smaller for larger sample sizes, all else being equal. From this it follows that 95 percent CIs become smaller, or narrower, for larger samples (again, all else being equal). To understand why, let's consider a thought experiment. Suppose we had 1,200 meals in our sample instead of 300. Our SE would then be calculated as:

$$\frac{318.672}{\sqrt{1200}} = 9.199 \approx 9.2.$$

The new margin of error becomes 18 (1.96 × 9.2 ≈ 18), which is about half of what it was previously (36). The much narrower 95 percent CI becomes:

$$522.7 \pm 1.96 \times 9.2 \rightarrow 522.7 \pm 18 = [504.7, 540.7].$$

This example illustrates a broader and important principle. When the sample size increases fourfold, the margin of error is reduced by 50 percent (from 36 to 18 in our case), resulting in a narrower or more precise 95 percent CI.[9] The implication is that we get to say more precise things about populations when we study larger samples from such populations, all else being equal. A corollary is that statistical associations or group differences more "easily" become statistically significant in larger samples.[10]

SPECIAL TOPIC 2: SIGNIFICANCE TESTING OF POPULATION DATA

Everything mentioned in this chapter applies to the classic scenario of analyzing a randomly selected sample from a large population. This, as mentioned earlier, is the default mode of statistics – or at least it used to be. Nowadays, researchers increasingly analyze population data directly. In fact, we have already analyzed population data earlier in this book: both the football player data and the biathlon data are population data.[11] But is it appropriate to use significance tests and p-values with population data? The issue is that we typically use a significance test and a p-value to assess whether it is likely that random differences between the sample and the population could have brought about the results we find in our sample. But in the case of population data there are no such differences because we are studying, well, the population per se.

There are two common approaches to this conundrum in current practice: (1) treat the population as a "random sample" from some imaginary superpopulation and perform tests of significance *as if* we are working on sample data in the usual sense or (2) abandon the idea of significance testing when analyzing population data. Personally, I have much sympathy for the second approach, but the first is by far the more popular choice among researchers today.[12] So, I'll continue to use significance tests and p-values for population data in what follows.

To provide more insight into my personal stance, though, let's reconsider the average number of matches played in the football data. The mean is 182, the SD is 109, and the number of players is 310. We calculate the SE in the normal manner, assuming (for the argument's sake) that the 310 players are a sample:

$$\frac{109}{\sqrt{310}} = 6.1908 \approx 6.2.$$

Fast-forward to the 95 percent CI ranging from roughly 170 to 194 matches. The question I find difficult to answer is this: to what population of football player does this CI apply? I have no satisfactory answer for this, hence my sympathy for the abandon-option when it comes to significance testing of population data.

KEY LEARNING POINTS

The key learning points in this chapter were:

- In research, we often study samples from much larger populations although the populations are of main interest. This practice is often grounded in practical or financial reasons.
- Assuming that our sample is representative of the unknown population under scrutiny, we may study the sample to get reliable, if not totally precise, answers for the population.
- The best, if not the only, strategy to obtain a representative sample is to perform random sampling, akin to mimicking a lottery.

- The statistical results we obtain for sample data are precise; the corresponding results for the unknown population are always approximate.
- We use 95 percent CIs to quantify the precision in our approximate assessment of populations.
- We employ a significance test to determine whether it is likely that random chance differences between our sample and the unknown population may account for the associations or group differences we find in our sample.
- If it is unlikely that random chance differences between our sample and the population can account for the association or group difference we find in our sample, we judge our finding to be "statistically significant."
- In statistics, "unlikely" in the point just above typically refers to a p-value of 5 percent or less as the main convention.
- Compared to smaller samples, larger samples allow for making more precise statements about the populations we are studying, all else being equal.
- Using tests of significance on population data is sometimes defensible – and sometimes more questionable.

NOTES

1 In many applications in current practice, we use more complicated techniques than simple random sampling (as in a lottery). Be that as it may, I find no reason to go into these in this introductory book. See the further reading section, especially Clark et al. (2021).

2 Some prefer to use $n - 1$ in the denominator. In large samples, this adjustment has little bearing on the (estimated) size of the SE. For samples smaller than about 120 units, we should multiply by a number somewhat larger than 1.96 to get the correct SE; cf. Agresti (2018, p. 127). For example, in a sample of 30 units, we should normally multiply by 2.042. In practice, you need not to worry about this when doing statistical analysis. Your statistics program does the necessary adjustments for you.

3 Like in endnote 2, we should for small samples ($n < 120$) multiply by a number somewhat larger than 1.96. As also mentioned in endnote 2, however, your statistics program makes the necessary adjustments for you.

4 Strictly speaking but venturing almost into the metaphysical: if we draw "indefinite" repeated samples of $n = 300$ in the exact same way and calculate the CI for each, 95 percent of these CIs would contain the true mean value of the total bill variable in the population. See Spiegelhalter (2019) for more technicalities on this.

5 You find the formula for this SE in Thrane (2022). Agresti (2018) is the source for all types of SEs.

6 Truth be told, we might commit two wrongdoings in significance testing. We might reject a true null hypothesis, or we might accept a false null hypothesis. The former is known as committing a Type I error, and the latter is committing a Type II error. While textbooks in statistics tend to make a big issue out of these possible wrongdoings, they rarely take up much page space in research papers, at least in my experience. In any event, see the further reading section. Another topic for the further reading section has to do with the power of a hypothesis test. Such power refers to the test's ability to detect a true alternative hypothesis. In other words, we are talking about its ability to identify an effect when one truly exists in the population. More power is to generally to be preferred, all else being equal.

7 The p-values I refer to in this book are the results of a so-called two-tailed test, which by far is the most common type of test. See the further reading section for the distinction between a one-tailed test and a two-tailed test.

8 The sample size is in the denominator in all formulas for computing the SE; cf. Agresti (2018).

9 See Agresti (2018).

10 The p-values decrease in magnitude due to smaller SEs in larger samples, all else being equal.

11 The beer data are not a full-fledged population. But they are, at least in my estimation, still more of a population than a sample.

12 Berk (2004) and Gorard (2021) are staunch defenders of the second abandon-significance-testing tradition in the presence of population data. (Gorard is also skeptical toward significance testing in general!) Spiegelhalter (2019) opts for significance testing by "acting like" the data were generated by some form of random process, akin to the superpopulation approach. There are other arguments for favoring the use of significance test on population data (e.g., Alexander, 2015), but I personally tend to find these a bit on the metaphysical side.

FURTHER READING

I recommend Agresti (2018), Freedman et al. (2007), Clark et al. (2021), and Thrane (2022) as follow-ups to this chapter. I also recommend Schneider (2013), Reinhart (2015), Gorard (2021), and Spiegelhalter (2019).

APPENDIX: A SHORT PRIMER ON THE CENTRAL LIMIT THEOREM (CLT)

Wheelan (2014, p. 127) calls the CLT "the Lebron James of statistics – if Lebron were also a supermodel, a Harvard professor, and the winner of the Nobel Peace Prize." His comparison is apt. Below, I lay out the key idea.

We use the properties of the normal distribution to estimate 95 percent CIs, to estimate acceptance regions for null hypotheses, and to perform significance tests. And we do all this *without* requiring the variables we are analyzing to be normally distributed themselves. This is all thanks to the CLT. The foundation of the CLT is the idea that a large, randomly drawn sample closely mirrors the population from which it is drawn. This is actually an informal way of expressing the so-called Law of Large Numbers. Let's look at our restaurant meal data again.

Based on the tip amount variable, we can easily create a dummy variable distinguishing between those diners who provided a tip and those who did not. Table 4.A.1 shows the frequency table results: 45 percent of the diners provided a tip. Obviously, this variable does not follow a normal distribution, because no variable with only two categories can ever be normally distributed!

Table 4.A.1 shows us the outcome when I drew one sample from my population of 750,000 meals and calculated the percentage of meals that included a tip. This percentage is 45, or 0.45 when expressed as a fraction. But just like in the main text, I did not stop there; I also drew 499 more samples and calculated the similar fraction for each of them. Table 4.A.2 lists the first six of these fractions, as well as the last one: fraction number 500. The histogram for all 500 fractions is displayed in Figure 4.A.1.

Figure 4.A.1 reveals a remarkable finding. Even though the tipping dummy variable obviously has no normal distribution in our first – and in real life: only – sample, its sampling distribution is

Table 4.A.1 Frequency table for the tipping variable. N = 300

Provided tip	Frequency	Frequency in percent	Cumulative percent
No	164	55	55
Yes	136	45	100

Table 4.A.2 Results of repeated sampling for the restaurant meal data

Sample number	Provided a tip: fraction
Sample 1	0.453
Sample 2	0.420
Sample 3	0.420
Sample 4	0.453
Sample 5	0.413
Sample 6	0.420
Sample …	…
Sample …	…
Sample 500	0.476

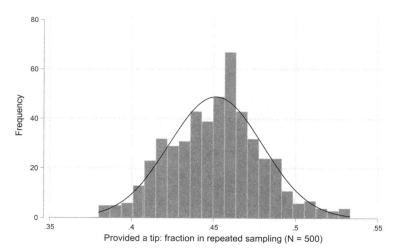

Figure 4.A.1 Histogram of "Provided a tip: fraction" in repeated sampling, with normal distribution superimposed

close to normally distributed around the average fraction of 0.45 (or 45 percent). If we were to repeat this process, say, 2,500 times, it *would be* perfectly, normally distributed. The takeaway message of the CLT is that we can use the normal distribution to calculate CIs and so on even when the variables in our sample are not normally distributed themselves. This is what we really are doing when we, as the saying goes, "invoke the CLT."

SEVERAL INDEPENDENT VARIABLES AND ONE DEPENDENT VARIABLE

Multiple regression

CHAPTER OVERVIEW

DOI: 10.4324/9781032640808-5

INTRODUCTION

While Chapter 3 explored *x-y* associations in a sample, Chapter 4 equipped us with the tools needed to determine if such sample associations were likely to be present in the population from which the sample was drawn. This chapter expands on Chapter 3 by examining how multiple independent variables (x_1, x_2, x_3, ...) *simultaneously* affect *y*. The motivation for this endeavor is straightforward. Rarely, if ever, is a real-life *y*-variable affected by only one *x*-variable. Moreover, some of these *x*-variables probably matter more than others, and it could be informative to identify when or if this is the case. The go-to solution in this situation is to perform *multiple* linear regression analysis.

Let's start with a thought experiment. Suppose you somehow have identified two dietary segments: the TWC group and the BWB group. While the TWC group consumes a lot of tap water (TW) and carrots (C), the BWB group drinks a lot of bottled water (BW) and eats a lot of bananas (B). Suppose further that the TWC group, on average, reports higher subjective well-being than the BWB group. Your task is to determine whether it is the tap water or the carrots that causes the higher level of subjective well-being in the TWC group. But as it stands, this question is impossible to answer. Yet if you were able to discern the tap water drinkers from the carrot eaters *within* the TWC group – essentially isolating these two subgroups – you could in principle answer your question. This, in essence, is what multiple regression analysis does.

MULTIPLE REGRESSION ANALYSIS: PRELIMINARIES

We associate *x* and *y* in bivariate regression. End of story. In multiple regression, we *simultaneously* associate x_1 and x_2 to *y*. Hence, multiple regression contains two or more independent variables or x-es. Using the notation introduced in the appendix to Chapter 3, we express the general multiple regression model as:

$$y = b_0 + b_1x_1 + b_2x_2 + b_3x_3 + \ldots + e.$$

But let's not get too caught up in technicalities. The crucial ability of multiple regression is to find the *relative* contribution of x_1, x_2, and x_3 (and so on) in terms of explaining variation in y. To revisit our caricature experiment, we could under the right circumstances use multiple regression to tease out the relative contribution of tap water drinking (x_1) and carrot eating (x_2) in explaining variation in subjective well-being. Now, let's apply this quantitative reasoning to real-life data. We return, not for the last time, to our football data.

The dependent variable, y, is the total number of matches played in career. The first independent variable, x_1, indicates whether a player has represented his national team (coded 1) or not (coded 0). We saw this example back in Table 3.3. The second independent variable, x_2, is the age of the player, as seen in Table 3.1. Using the notation where b_1 corresponds to x_1 and b_2 corresponds to x_2, these regression equations were:

$$\text{Total number of football matches} = b_0 + b_1 \text{national team representation},$$

and

$$\text{Total number of football matches} = b_0 + b_2 \text{age of player}.$$

The results from these bivariate regression models re-appear in columns A and B in Table 5.1. To recap: players with representation for their national teams have, on average, played about 95 more matches in their career than players without such representation (column A). In addition, a player who is, say, 31 years of age has played 23 more matches in his career on average than a player who is 30 years of age (column B). Both bivariate regression coefficients are statistically significant at the 0.001 level, if we consider this relevant for these population data.

The results in column C stem from the multiple regression:

$$\text{Total number of football matches} = b_0 + b_1 \text{national team representation} + b_2 \text{age of player}.$$

The first thing to note about the multiple regression in column C is that the coefficient for the national team representation dummy is considerably smaller than in the bivariate regression: 28 versus 95. The key to understand multiple regression lies in this comparison.

In column A, national team players and players with no national representation are compared with respect to the average of the total matches in career variable. That is, the two groups are compared *without* taking any other features of these players into account. In the multiple regression in column C, however, these two groups are compared while also taking the age of the players into account. This mysterious "into account" is a mathematical procedure beyond the scope of this book. Metaphorically, you can think of it as comparing national team players and non-national team players being of the *same* age. And when doing this, we find that national team players have played 28 more matches in their career than players with no representation for their national teams.

Why this large reduction in the national team coefficient? There must be something going on behind the scenes, right? Absolutely. On average, players with representation for their national teams are three years older than players with no such representation. These means are, respectively, 28 years and 25 years. This age difference implies that when we compare the two groups in the bivariate regression, we are comparing an older representation group to a younger non-representation group. Much of the 95-match difference can in this way be attributed to the age difference between the two groups. The multiple regression effectively takes this group difference in age "out of the equation," so to speak. What remains is an

Table 5.1 Total number of matches played by independent variables. Bivariate linear regressions (A and B) and multiple linear regressions (C and D)

Independent variables	A	B	C	D
National team (no = 0; yes = 1)	94.71★★★ (14.99)	–	28.21★★★ (7.64)	27.91★★★ (7.62)
Age of player	–	22.90★★★ (0.69)	22.17★★★ (0.71)	22.26★★★ (0.71)
Footed (right = 0; left/both = 1)	–	–	–	−11.01 (6.51)
Constant	164.09	−403.24	−389.92	−389.23
R^2	0.115	0.779	0.789	0.791
N	310	310	310	310

Note. Standard errors are in parentheses.

★ $p < 0.05$; ★★ $p < 0.01$; ★★★ $p < 0.001$ (two-tailed tests).

age-*adjusted* group difference: 28 matches. We refer to this adjusted regression coefficient as the *unique* or *partial* effect of the *x*-variable in question.[1]

What makes this example relevant for other settings is that we often face situations where there are associations among the independent variables – as in the case with the national team representation dummy (x_1) and age of player (x_2). Truth be told, this is the rule rather than the exception in the kinds of data we have examined in this book. From this it follows that whenever we aim to find the unique effect of x_1 on *y*, we need to adjust it for the effect of x_2. A convenient feature of multiple regression is that this principle works in reverse as well: when the regression coefficient of x_1 is adjusted for the regression coefficient of x_2, the regression coefficient of x_2 is simultaneously adjusted for the regression coefficient of x_1.

Running a multiple regression in a statistics program is as straightforward as running a bivariate one. It is simply a matter of instructing the program to add this or that extra *x*-variable into the regression model. What changes is the interpretation of the regression coefficient or *effect*. Take for example the national team representation dummy in column C. The interpretation of this variable's regression coefficient or effect now reads: statistically adjusted for the effect of players' age, players with national team representation have played 28 more matches in their career than players with no national team representation. We often use phrases like "controlled for …" or "holding … constant" or "ceteris paribus" in this context, all of which essentially meaning the same thing. That is why the terms partial or unique regression coefficients or effects are often used when discussing the results of multiple regression analysis.

Does this stop at x_1 and x_2? Of course not. The mathematical principle applies equally to 3, 5 and, possibly, 367 independent variables or *x*-es. Column D in Table 5.1 adds the dummy footedness or x_3 to the regression model in column C. Players are either right-footed (coded 0) or left/both-footed (coded 1). Little happens to the effects of the national team dummy and age when footedness is added to the regression. Left/both-footed players have played 11 fewer matches than right-footed players. More precisely, statistically adjusted for the effects of national team representation and players' age, left/both-footed players have played 11 fewer matches than right-footed ones. Yet this coefficient is not significant at $p < 0.05$, with a *t*-value of −1.69 (-11.01/6.51 = −1.69). Now, let's move on to one of our familiar case studies.

CASE STUDY 1: THE TYPICAL QUANTITATIVE CHARACTERISTICS OF PIZZA RESTAURANT MEALS, CONT.

Let's cut directly to the chase. The research question is how three *x*-variables − presence of alcohol with the meal, number of diners, and number of orders − affect the total bill for the meal. To make this example more instructive, we go about examining it in a step-by-step manner. Table 5.2 presents the results.

We begin with column A in Table 5.2. On average, meals that include alcohol cost NOK 81 more in total than meals that do not include alcohol. Albeit being statistically significant at the 0.05 level, the alcohol variable does not explain much of the variation in the total bill (R^2 = 1 percent). Moving on to the multiple regression in column B, the alcohol variable's effect increases when controlled for number of diners.[2] Statistically adjusted for the effect of number of diners, meals that include alcohol cost NOK 106 more in total than meals that do not include alcohol. In addition, statistically adjusted for the effect of the alcohol variable, one more diner at the table entails a NOK 127 increase in the total bill. Or to be more precise: a four-person table pays NOK 127 more than a three-person table. Both multiple

Table 5.2 Total bill for meal by independent variables. Bivariate linear regression (A) and multiple linear regressions (B and C)

Independent variables	A	B	C
Alcohol with meal (no = 0; yes = 1)	81.23* (39.45)	106.14*** (31.26)	92.17*** (24.48)
Number of diners	−	126.70*** (9.46)	76.99*** (8.24)
Number of orders	−	−	49.75*** (3.62)
Constant	497.22	173.10	15.99
R^2	0.01	0.385	0.625
N	300	300	300

Note. Standard errors are in parentheses.

* $p < 0.05$; ** $p < 0.01$; *** $p < 0.001$ (two-tailed tests).

regression coefficients are statistically significant at the 0.001 level, and combined they explain almost 40 percent of the variation in the total bill. The huge increase in R^2 suggests that the number of diners variable explains more of the variation in the total bill than the alcohol variable.

Column C has all three x-variables in the regression. Statistically adjusted for the effects of number of diners and number of orders, meals that include alcohol cost NOK 92 more in total than meals that not include alcohol. The effect of number of diners decreases when adjusted for number or orders, going from NOK 127 in column B to NOK 77 in column C. Lastly, statistically adjusted for the effects of the alcohol variable and the number of diners variable, one more order at the table entails a NOK 50 increase in the total bill. Or to be more precise: a seven-order table pays NOK 50 more than a six-order table. The R^2 value informs us that the three x-variables together explain almost 63 percent of the variation in the total bill variable.[3] All three partial or unique regression coefficients are statistically significant at the 0.001 level.

Figure 5.1 is based on the regression model in column C and shows the effects of the alcohol dummy and the number of orders variable.

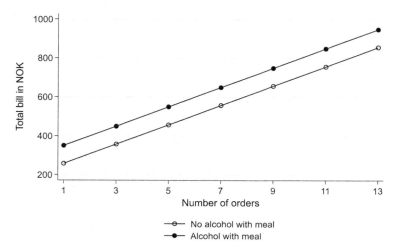

Figure 5.1 The effect of alcohol with meal and number of orders on total bill, based on the regression model in column C in Table 5.2

The NOK 92 distance or gap between the parallel regression lines corresponds to the regression coefficient for the alcohol dummy. The upward sloping lines show the effect of an increasing number of orders, corresponding to the regression coefficient of NOK 49.75. A similar stylistic plot (a plot without data points) can also be made with the number of diners variable on the x-axis. But you get the picture without getting it from me!

MULTIPLE REGRESSION WITH NOMINAL X-VARIABLES HAVING MORE THAN TWO CATEGORIES

The nominal x-variables we have examined in this chapter have only had two categories, making them dummy variables. Yet many real-world nominal x-variables have more than two categories.

The trick to remember in such situations is that when an x-variable has two categories, A or B, it gets represented by *one* coefficient in a regression. This is the familiar dummy variable case where the regression coefficient is the mean difference in y between categories A and B. However, when an x-variable has three categories, as in A, B, or C, it gets represented by *two* coefficients: one for the y-difference between A and B and another for the y-difference between A and C. Once we know the y-differences between A and B and A and C, we also implicitly know the y-difference between A and C. (Similarly, four categories would imply three coefficients, and so on.)

Let's revisit our football data and the player position variable having four categories: defender, midfielder, winger, and striker. The dependent variable, y, is the total number of goals scored in career (mean = 23; min = 0, max = 191; SD = 27). In other words, the research question is how the position variable affects the goal-scoring variable. Table 5.3 takes us through the particulars.

Since there are four player positions, we end up with three regression coefficients. The key to unlock the results in column A lies in the fact that we created one dummy for each position: defender (no or yes), midfielder (no or yes), winger (no or yes), and striker (no or yes). But then we instructed our statistics program to include only three of these four dummies in the regression model, yielding three coefficients. The dummy not included in the regression now acts as the reference group and is represented by the constant.[4]

Column A shows that, on average, midfielders have scored 6.70 more goals than defenders in their careers, while defenders, represented by the constant, have scored 11.40 goals. Similarly, wingers and strikers have scored 18.62 and 40.72 more goals, respectively, than defenders. The mean difference in goals scored by, say, wingers and strikers is 22 goals ($40.72 - 18.62 = 22.10$).

Column B shows some changes to these player position effects caused by the addition of the players' age as another x-variable in the regression. The interpretation follows the usual setup: adjusted for the effect of age, midfielders have scored 10.93 more goals than defenders, and so on for the remaining positions, with the differences being 23.03 and 41.92 goals. Unsurprisingly, we also find a positive age effect. Adjusted for the effects of player position, a 25-year-old player has scored 3.36 more goals in his career than a 24-year-old player. Player nationality is added to the regression model in column C. Adjusted for the effects of player position and age, a foreign player has scored 5.01 less goals than a Norwegian player.

Table 5.3 Number of goals in career by independent variables. Multiple linear regressions

Independent variables	A	B	C
Player position[a]			
Midfielder (= 1)	6.70★	10.93★★★	11.00★★★
	(3.20)	(2.52)	(2.50)
Winger (= 1)	18.62★★★	23.03★★★	23.11★★★
	(3.62)	(2.86)	(2.84)
Striker (= 1)	40.72★★★	41.92★★★	42.43★★★
	(3.86)	(3.02)	(3.01)
Age	–	3.36★★★	3.34★★★
		(0.24)	(0.24)
Nationality (Norwegian = 0; foreign = 1)	–	–	−5.01★
			(2.16)
Constant	11.40	−76.64	−74.57
R^2	0.284	0.562	0.570
N	310	310	310

Note. Standard errors are in parentheses.

[a] Reference = Defender.

★ $p < 0.05$; ★★ $p < 0.01$; ★★★ $p < 0.001$ (two-tailed tests).

CASE STUDY 2: WOMEN'S SPRINT BIATHLON IN THE OLYMPICS, CONT.

The y-variable is total race time in minutes from start to finish, akin to in Table 2.6 and Figure 3.4. The x-variables include the skiers' continent of origin, year of games, and the total number of hits on target. And the research question we are exploring is how these variables are associated. Table 5.4 presents the results of this regression model in which two of the x-variables are nominal with more than two categories each.

For convenience, I now displace with the "statistically adjusted for …" phrase. Nordic skiers spent almost half a minute (0.48 min) *less* on a race than European skiers (the reference group). Skiers from Asia or Oceania spent 0.58 minutes more on a race than European skiers. Finally, the race time difference between skiers from America and Europe was 0.75 minutes. Nordic skiers were the

Table 5.4 Total race time by independent variables. Multiple linear regression

Independent variables	
Skiers' continent of origin[a]	
Nordic countries: Finland, Sweden, or Norway (= 1)	$-0.48 \ (0.159)$★★
Asia or Oceania (= 1)	$0.58 \ (0.144)$★★★
America (= 1)	$0.75 \ (0.171)$★★★
Year of game[b]	
2006 games (= 1)	$1.62 \ (0.174)$★★★
2010 games (= 1)	$-1.44 \ (0.174)$★★★
2014 games (= 1)	$-0.31 \ (0.175)$
2018 games (= 1)	$-0.53 \ (0.172)$★★
2022 games (= 1)	$-0.19 \ (0.170)$
Number of hits on target	$-0.62 \ (0.035)$★★★
Constant	28.50
R^2	0.614
N	501

Note. Standard errors are in parentheses.

[a] Reference = European continent.

[b] Reference = Year 2002 games.

★ $p < 0.05$; ★★ $p < 0.01$; ★★★ $p < 0.001$ (two-tailed tests).

fastest, followed by the European skiers, as a longer race time implies skiing at a slower pace. Skiers from America were the slowest.

Compared with the 2002 games (the reference), the race in the 2006 games was 1.62 minutes slower. Conversely, the race in the 2010 games was 1.44 minutes faster than the 2002 games. The games most similar in terms of race time were those in 2014 and 2022, with a difference of only 0.12 min $(0.31-0.19 = 0.12)$. The regression coefficient for the number of hits on target is -0.62. This suggests that skiers who hit, say, eight targets had race times that were 0.62 minute, or about 37 seconds, faster than the skiers who hit seven targets.

INTERACTION EFFECTS

As a first brush stroke or default-mode in statistical analysis, we tend to assume that the association between x and y is consistent across all subgroups in our data. This is a simplification done for two reasons. First, statistical models are easier to compute in the mathematical sense when assuming "effect similarity." Second, statistical results are easier to communicate to audiences when assuming such similarity. Even so, and perhaps more often than we are aware of, assuming that the effect of x on y is similar for subgroups A and B in the data might not sync well with reality. In other words, the association between x and y could in real life be stronger for the units in subgroup A and weaker for the units in subgroup B, or vice versa. When this happens, we are dealing with *interaction* effects.

Formally speaking, an interaction effect occurs when the magnitude of the effect of x_1 on y is dependent on the value of x_2. So, if a regression coefficient is 2.5 for subgroup A and 0.5 for subgroup B in our data, we are on the trace of an interaction effect. This is because the magnitude of the regression coefficient is contingent on which subgroup we are examining. But this stuff is much easier to get a grip on using an example. We return to a case study.

CASE STUDY 3: THE PRICE, QUALITY RATING, AND ALCOHOL CONTENT OF BEERS, CONT.

Figure 5.2 presents a scatterplot between the bottle price and the alcohol content of our beers along with a regression line.

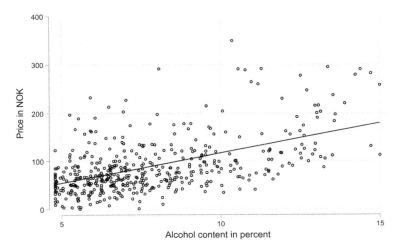

Figure 5.2 Scatterplot of bottle price and alcohol content of beers, with linear regression line

The coefficient for the regression line is 12.48 (not shown), suggesting that a beer with an alcohol content of 8 percent costs NOK 12.48 more on average than a beer with an alcohol content of 7 percent. Figure 5.2 is a default regression assuming that all subgroups in the data have the "same" regression coefficient. In our case, this implies that the regression coefficient is assumed to be the same for both US and Swedish beers, which we know are the beer nationalities present in the data. But is this equal-coefficient scenario necessarily accurate in real life?

To answer this question in a preliminary fashion, Figure 5.3 splits the data for the two countries into two subgroups and plots the corresponding regression lines. A clear picture emerges. The regression line for the US beers is steeper than the corresponding regression line for the Swedish beers. Not shown, the regression coefficients yielding the two lines are 13.01 (the USA) and 6.71 (Sweden). Figure 5.3 shows an interaction effect; the magnitude of the effect of alcohol content (x_1) on bottle price (y) is dependent on the value (the USA or Sweden) of the beers' production country (x_2).

Since many real-life variable associations are conditional in some way, interaction effects – or conditional variable associations, as they

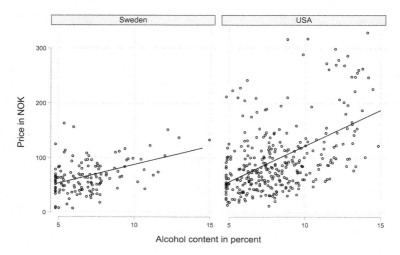

Figure 5.3 Scatterplot of bottle price and alcohol content of beers by production country, with linear regression lines

also are known – are common in the behavioral and social sciences.
They are typically presented graphically as stylistic effects without
data points, as seen in Figure 5.4. The regression results yielding
Figure 5.4 are displayed in Table 5.5. The non-parallel regression
lines in the figure express the interaction effect, with the steeper line
for US beers. In contrast, parallel regression lines (as in Figure 5.1
some paragraphs back) suggest no interaction effect. But how do
we determine whether non-parallel regression lines are more in
sync with reality than parallel regression lines? Table 5.5 answers
this question as well.

Table 5.5 includes the *x*-variables production country, alcohol
content, and the *product term* of production country and alcohol content as symbolized by a multiplication sign. (Creating a
product term variable is a straightforward doing in any statistics
program.) The key to unlock the interaction effect lies in the coding of the dummy variable. Since the country dummy is coded 0
for Sweden and 1 for the USA, the alcohol content coefficient
applies to Swedish beers. This coefficient is 6.71: Swedish beers
with an alcohol content of 8 percent cost NOK 6.71 more than
Swedish beers with an alcohol content of 7 percent. To find the

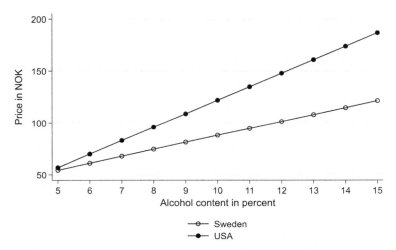

Figure 5.4 The effect of alcohol content on beer bottle price, based on regression model in Table 5.5

equivalent coefficient for US beers, we add the coefficient for the product term to the Swedish coefficient: $6.71 + 6.30 = 13.01$. In this way, US beers with an alcohol content of 8 percent cost NOK 13.01 more than US beers with an alcohol content of 7 percent. The larger regression coefficient yields a steeper regression line for US beers.

How can we determine if an interaction regression model – a model with non-parallel regression lines – is more in sync with real life than the plain-vanilla model with parallel regression lines? There are four pointers. First, the coefficient for the product term should differ from zero, as it does in our example. If the coefficient is near zero, this suggests parallel regression lines being more in sync with reality. Second, the coefficient for the product term should be statistically significant, as it is in our example. Third, the R^2 value for the interaction regression model should be larger than the R^2 value for the plain-vanilla regression model. It is in our example, although Table 5.5 does not show this. Fourth and finally, non-parallel regression lines should make some kind of theoretical or common sense. They might just do that in our example, but that is a (beer) story for another time or book.

Table 5.5 Beer bottle price by independent variables. Multiple linear regression

Independent variables	
Production country (Sweden = 0, USA = 1)	−29.08 (16.40)
Alcohol content (in percent)	6.71 (1.98)★★
Production country × alcohol content	6.30 (2.21)★★
Constant	20.95
R^2	0.332
N	462

Note. Standard errors are in parentheses.

★ $p < 0.05$; ★★ $p < 0.01$; ★★★ $p < 0.001$ (two-tailed tests).

INTERACTION EFFECTS IN STATISTICAL ANALYSIS: GENERAL THOUGHTS

Whenever a regression includes two x-variables, x_1 and x_2, there might be an interaction effect present: the regression coefficient for the product term $x_1 \times x_2$. It follows that a regression model containing, say, ten x-variables has an almost endless list of possible product terms. (Every x can be multiplied by the other nine x-es.) The advice stemming from this knowledge is that we test for interaction effects only when we have some theoretical expectation that two x-variables will yield a significant interaction effect. But there are exceptions to this "rule." For instance, when analyzing questionnaire data, it is often far-sighted to examine whether x-y associations are similar for both sexes. (A case study illustration is coming up later.) Similar reasoning applies to all sorts of data sets having several "large" subgroups.

The interaction effect above was between a dummy variable (production country) and a quantitative variable (alcohol content). That was a pedagogical choice on my part. Still, there might be similar interactions for all sorts of variables regardless of their measurement level. The most common combinations in addition to the one we just saw are between two dummies or two quantitative variables. No worries, all statistics programs solve the practicalities of making product terms of these variables as well.

CASE STUDY 4: THE WELL-BEING OF NORWEGIANS, CONT.

Visiting the doctor is a routine part of most people's lives, though the frequency of these visits varies greatly. Obviously, this is true among Norwegians as well. Our research question is to explore how the x-variables presence of any long-lasting illnesses or health problems ("troubles"), biological sex, and age affect the number of times a year one visits a doctor (mean = 2.56; min = 0; max = 12; SD = 2.87).[5] The plain-vanilla or non-interaction regression appears in column A in Table 5.6.

Column A says that respondents suffering from long-lasting troubles visit the doctor 1.91 more times per year than those not suffering from such troubles. (I keep displacing with the "statistically adjusted for …" phrase.) Additionally, women visit the doctor 0.76 more times per year than men. The negative age effect suggests that older people visit the doctor less frequently than younger people. Figure 5.5 visualizes the effects of sex and age based on the non-interaction regression in column A. We notice two downward sloping but parallel regression lines, suggesting that doctor visits tend to be fewer among older people, and that women generally visit the doctor more often than men.

Table 5.6 Number of doctor visits per year by independent variables. Multiple regressions

Independent variables	A	B
Long-lasting illnesses or health problems (no = 0; yes = 1)	1.91★★★ (0.071)	1.92★★★ (0.071)
Sex (male = 0; female = 1)	0.76★★★ (0.068)	2.50★★★ (0.212)
Age (in years)	−0.009★★★ (0.002)	0.009★★★ (0.003)
Sex × Age	–	−0.039★★★ (0.004)
Constant	1.90	1.06
R^2	0.125	0.135
N	6,310	6,310

Note. Standard errors are in parentheses.

★ $p < 0.05$; ★★ $p < 0.01$; ★★★ $p < 0.001$ (two-tailed tests).

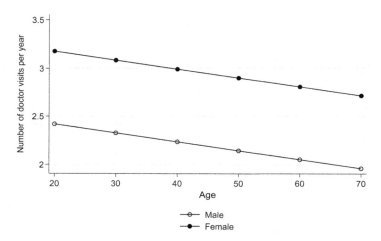

Figure 5.5 The effect of biological sex and age on number of doctor visits per year, based on column A in Table 5.6. Note that the *y*-axis is truncated, starting at two visits per year

Now for the results in column B in Table 5.6, which also include a product term for the variables sex and age. The key to unlock the interaction effect is again to notice the coding of the dummy variable. Since men are coded 0, the age effect applies to men. The small, positive age coefficient (0.009) suggests that older men visit the doctor slightly *more* frequently than younger men. To find the analogous age coefficient for women, we add the regression coefficient for the product term to men's age coefficient: $0.009 + (-0.039) = -0.030$. This implies that older women visit the doctor *less* frequently than younger women. Figure 5.6 shows this interaction effect more vividly than any words can provide.

This example offers a cautionary tale. The interaction model in column B tells a different story about the doctor visits of men and women than the non-interaction model in column A. When choosing between the two competing regression models yielding the differing stories, the evaluation criteria mentioned some paragraphs back favor the interaction model. Moreover, common sense supports this model too, as many women in their 20s and 30s visit the doctor more frequently due to pregnancies.

But we are not finished yet! The regressions in Table 5.6 implicitly assume that the age effect is linear for both sexes. But is this necessarily the case in real life? Not at all. The regression that generated Figure 5.7 (not shown) relaxes this assumption and calculates non-linear regression lines for both sexes. We can see that while the age effect for men

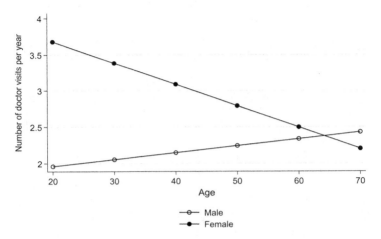

Figure 5.6 The effect of biological sex and age on number of doctor visits per year, based on column B in Table 5.6. Note that the y-axis is truncated, starting at two visits per year

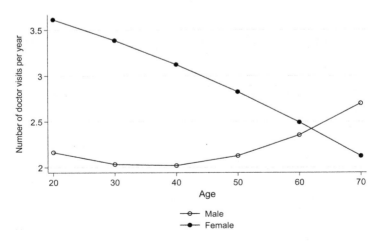

Figure 5.7 The effect of biological sex and age on number of doctor visits per year, based on model B in Table 5.6 as well as a squared term for the age variable

has a slight U-bend, the age effect for woman becomes (slightly) more negative for older ages. Also, by the age of 70 years, men clearly visit the doctor clearly more frequently than women. So, we are dealing with a combination of a non-linear effect and an interaction effect. But let's not delve deeper into this now.

INTERACTIONS BETWEEN TWO DUMMY X-VARIABLES

Let's return to our football data. Once again, the dependent variable is the total number of matches played in career. The first independent variable, x_1, denotes whether a player is of Norwegian nationality (coded 0) or foreign nationality (coded 1). The second independent variable, x_2, indicates whether a player has played for his national team (coded 1) or not (coded 0). Column A in Table 5.7 presents the linear multiple regression, assuming no interaction effect.

Discarding the "adjusted for ..." phrase, we find that foreign players have played 43 *fewer* matches in their career than Norwegian players. Similarly, players with representation for their national teams have played 105 more matches than players without such representation. This regression model's constant also has a real-life equivalent: the average total number of matches played by Norwegian players with no representation for their national team. This number is 175. (The constant refers to the units for which both x_1 and $x_2 = 0$.)

Table 5.7 Total number of matches played by independent variables. Multiple regressions

Independent variables	A	B
Nationality (Norwegian = 0; foreign = 1)	−43★★ (13)	−19 (14)
National team (no = 0; yes = 1)	105★★★ (15)	151★★★ (20)
Nationality × national team	–	−103★★ (30)
Constant	175	169
R^2	0.146	0.178
N	310	310

Note. Standard errors are in parentheses.

★ $p < 0.05$; ★★ $p < 0.01$; ★★★ $p < 0.001$ (two-tailed tests).

Column B in Table 5.7 displays the interaction effect regression. Once again, the key lies in the coding of the nationality dummy. Since Norwegians are coded 0, the national team representation effect refers to Norwegians. Norwegians with representation for their national team have played 151 more matches than Norwegians without such representation. To find the analogous regression coefficient for foreign players, we add the coefficient for the product term to the Norwegians' coefficient: $151 + (-103) = 48$. This suggests that foreign players with representation for national teams have played 48 more matches than foreign players without such representation. National team representation has, in other words, a *larger* effect for Norwegian players than it has for foreign players. This interaction effect is shown in Figure 5.8. We notice the steeper "regression line" among the Norwegian players.

The y-variables in this chapter have all been quantitative variables, which I previously said was a requirement for doing linear regression.[6] This was only partly true, sorry about that! In fact, linear regression, or some close cousin of it, can be used to analyze y-variables at all measurement levels, which of course contributes to its popularity. Most of these more advanced regression techniques

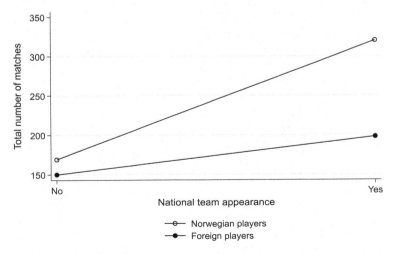

Figure 5.8 The effect of nationality and national team representation on total number of matches played, based on column B in Table 5.7. Note that the y-axis is truncated, starting at 150 matches

are for the further reading section, but there is one important special case that fits well within the traditional framework we have been using so far: the dummy dependent variable.

A DUMMY DEPENDENT VARIABLE/Y: THE LPM

Many y-variables in the social and behavioral sciences represent choices between something or nothing, or between A or B. We are talking about a binary choice. On many occasions, however, it should read "choice" as in for example survey questions tapping information on topics that have little or nothing to do with free choices. Such binary (choice) variables are what we have referred to as dummy variables in this book so far, only now these dummies serve as our dependent variables or y-s.

Applying linear regression on a dummy y has a name: the LPM or Linear Probability Model. Nothing changes in terms of practicalities; we give the statistics program the same instructions as before. The changes concern the interpretation of the regression coefficients because the y-variable now has only two values: 0 or 1. Let's look at some examples starting with our football data.

We have previously analyzed whether a football player has represented his national team (coded 1) or not (coded 0), but mostly as an x-variable. According to Table 3.5, 19 percent of the players have represented their national team. This dummy is now our y-variable. Our research question is whether player nationality and age affect national team representation. However, since such representation is a dummy variable, our question essentially becomes: do nationality and age affect the *probability of* having played for a national team? The resulting regression appears in Table 5.8.

The key to interpret the LPM is to understand what the regression coefficient implies. The first thing to remember is that the interpretation is done with respect to $y = 1$, namely the probability of having represented a national team in our example. The second thing to notice is that we are concerned with changes in probabilities as measured in percentage points. That settled, we are ready to begin. Adjusted for the effect of age, a foreign player has an 18 percentage points (0.178) higher probability of having represented his national team than a Norwegian player. Similarly, adjusted for the effect of player nationality, a 25-year-old player has an almost 3 percentage points (0.027) higher probability of having represented his national team than a 24-year-old player. Figure 5.9 visualizes these two effects.

Table 5.8 and Figure 5.9 both tell and show a translucent story. But they also highlight a limitation of the LPM. Consider the 18-year-old and 20-year-old Norwegian players. Both groups have *negative* probabilities of having represented their national teams,

Table 5.8 National team representation by independent variables. Multiple regression. Linear probability model (LPM)

Independent variables	
Nationality (Norwegian = 0; foreign = 1)	0.178★★★
	(0.045)
Age	0.027★★★
	(0.005)
Constant	−0.55
R^2	0.116
N	310

Note. Standard errors are in parentheses.

★ $p < 0.05$; ★★ $p < 0.01$; ★★★ $p < 0.001$ (two-tailed tests).

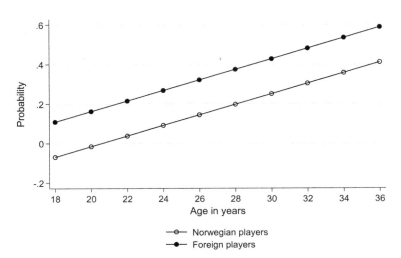

Figure 5.9 The effect of player nationality and age on the probability of having played for a national team, based on the results in Table 5.8

which is obviously impossible because probabilities are bounded between 0 and 1 or 0 and 100 percent. For this reason and a few others, some people are skeptical about the LPM. They prefer a regression model ensuring that probabilities always fall within the 0–1 range. Please say welcome to logistic regression analysis!

A DUMMY DEPENDENT VARIABLE/Y: MULTIPLE LOGISTIC REGRESSION

To cut a long story short and without delving into technical details (see the further reading section), the logistic regression model forces the probability of $y = 1$ to be in the range between 0 and 100 percent. Apart from this, running this regression model in any statistics program is as straightforward as running the basic, plain-vanilla model. Figure 5.10 is the logistic counterpart of Figure 5.9. There are, as expected, no probabilities below zero.[7]

Dummy y-variables are abundant in the social and behavioral sciences, and they show up in studies at least as often as quantitative y-variables. Coming straight up − no rest for the wicked! − is a classic example from labor market research.

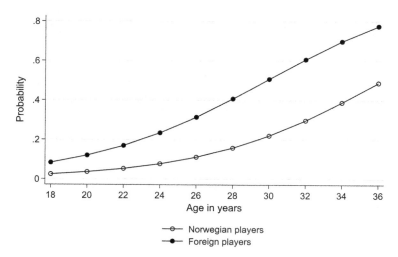

Figure 5.10 The effect of player nationality and age on the probability of having played for a national team, based on a multiple *logistic* regression analysis (not shown in a table)

CASE STUDY 4: THE WELL-BEING OF NORWEGIANS, CONT.

Most adult people in Norway are full-time employed. This can be thought of as a dummy variable: full-time employed or not full-time employed. About 65 percent of the respondents in our Norwegian sample are full-time employed (coded 1), leaving 35 percent in the not full-time employed category (coded 0). Our research question is to examine how certain x-variables affect the probability of being full-time employed. The LPM coming up with the answers is displayed in Table 5.9. (For convenience, I continue displacing with the "statistically adjusted for …" phrase.)

The first thing of note is that people with any long-lasting health troubles have a 15 percentage points (-0.146) lower probability of being full-time employed than people without such troubles. Similarly, smokers have a 6 percentage points (-0.058) lower probability of being full-time employed than non-smokers. In the same manner, while women are 15 percentage points less likely than men to be

Table 5.9 Full-time employment by independent variables. Multiple regression. Linear probability model (LPM)

Independent variables	
Long-lasting illnesses or health problems (no = 0; yes = 1)	-0.146 (0.010)★★★
Smoker (no = 0; yes = 1)	-0.058 (0.013)★★★
Sex (male = 0; female = 1)	-0.152 (0.010)★★★
Nationality (Norwegian = 0; foreign = 1)	-0.064 (0.012)★★★
Education level[a]	
Secondary level (= 1)	0.081 (0.014)★★★
Tertiary level (= 1)	0.175 (0.014)★★★
Age	0.083 (0.002)★★★
Age-squared (× 100)	-0.010 (0.002)★★★
Constant	-0.860
R^2	0.284
N	6,533

Note. Standard errors are in parentheses.

[a] Reference = Primary education level.

★ $p < 0.05$; ★★ $p < 0.01$; ★★★ $p < 0.001$ (two-tailed tests).

full-time employed, the similar difference between foreigners and Norwegians is just north of 6 percentage points. Norwegians are more often full-time employed than foreigners.

As for education, respondents with a tertiary education level have a 17.5 percentage points larger probability of being full-time employed than people with primary education (the reference group). The similar difference between the primary level and the secondary level is 8 percentage points. The effect of age is captured by the age variable and its squared value. The positive age coefficient and the negative age-squared coefficient suggest an inverted U-pattern between age and the probability of being full-time employed. (Figure 3.7 showed the same basic pattern.) This inverted U-bend is displayed in Figure 5.11 for men and women separately. We get to see that 40-year-olds have the highest probability of being full-time employed.

The results in Table 5.9 and Figure 5.11 assume no interaction effects between the x-variables. This is unlikely. For example, we might expect the age trajectories in terms of employment to vary between people with or without long-lasting health troubles. Allowing for such differences in the regression model (results not shown),

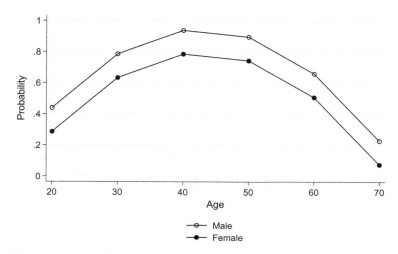

Figure 5.11 The effect of age and sex on the probability of being full-time employed, based on the results in Table 5.9

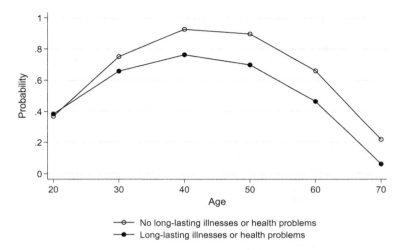

Figure 5.12 The effect of age on the probability of being full-time employed for two different health problem groups, based on the regression in Table 5.9 and product terms between the health problem variable and the two age variables

Figure 5.12 shows this to be the case: the differences in employment probabilities between the health trouble groups are largest in middle age, as understood between roughly 40 and 60 years of age.

The last point on the agenda for this chapter concerns a regression procedure with a certain magic-bullet flavor. This procedure applies to y-variables that can take on only positive values: prices, earnings (among the employed), and how often one engages in an activity among the doers of that activity. Essentially, we are talking about y-variables for which the value of zero cannot be observed – either in principle or in the case at hand.

SPECIAL TOPIC 1: LOGGING THE DEPENDENT VARIABLE/Y

Figure 5.13 is derived from a data set containing information on 121 TVs. While we have the price of the TVs on the y-axis, the size of the TVs is on the x-axis. The trend line is data-driven, meaning the line that best summarizes the association between the variables according to the data themselves. Two things are of notice: (1) There is a positive association between the variables; larger TVs are generally pricier than smaller TVs on average. No surprise there. (2) There is a non-linear association between the two variables; the effect of size on price is greater among the larger TVs. But since this non-linearity does not have a minimum or maximum inflection point, we cannot describe it as a U-bend or inverted U-bend. The solution to this problem is *not* to try and create a regression line with an increasing slope. Instead, the solution is to transform the y-variable.

So, what exactly is a variable transformation? A simple example illustrates this concept well. Suppose we want to convert TV prices from Norwegian Krone (NOK) to, say, Swedish ones (SEK). If so, we tell our statistics program to create a new variable in the following spirit:

generate price_SEK = price_NOK × 0.97,

because NOK 1 is the equivalent of SEK 0.97.

This procedure illustrates the crux of a variable transformation: (1) We have an original variable with plain-vanilla numbers as numerical

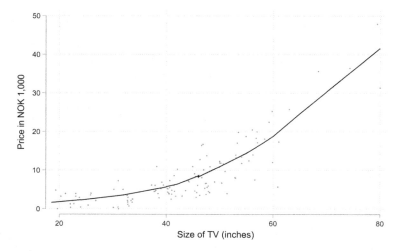

Figure 5.13 Scatterplot of TV price and size of TV, with data-driven trend line

values. (2) We apply some kind of mathematical formula to this variable. (3) We end up with a new variable with transformed values.

The mathematical formula of interest for our purposes is the natural logarithm, which is a great candidate for the further reading section. We apply this natural logarithm formula to the y-variable – which in the lingo reads as "logging y," hence the title of this section – to create a new variable called ln y. The match-up between some original numbers and their natural logarithms appears in Table 5.10. (To find the natural logarithm of a number on my calculator, I simply press the "ln" button followed by the number I want to convert. I bet the setup is rather similar on your calculator.)

What makes the variable transformations in Table 5.1 special is, essentially, that the distances between the original numbers are much smaller on the logarithmic scale. For instance, while 20 is 10 twice, 2.99 is not the double amount of 2.30. Similarly, while 1,000,000 is 10 times 100,000, 13.18 is only slightly more than 11.51. In short, large numbers are pulled closer to smaller numbers on the logarithmic scale. This mathematical property comes in handy for linearizing non-linear relationships, as shown in Figure 5.14 below. Figure 5.14 is akin to Figure 5.13 in all respects but one: the original price variable has been replaced with its natural logarithm (Ln). This substitution has an eye-catching consequence, namely that the association between the two variables becomes linear. As a result, we can use plain-vanilla linear regression to describe the linear association between the variables. Column A in Table 5.11 presents the regression results in question.

Table 5.10 Numbers and numbers expressed in natural logarithms

Original number/value		Natural logarithm value (Ln)
1	← →	0
10	← →	2.30
20	← →	2.99
100	← →	4.60
1,000	← →	6.90
10,000	← →	9.21
100,000	← →	11.51
1,000,000	← →	13.82

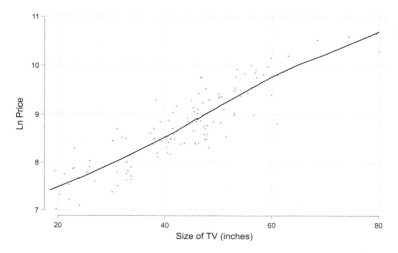

Figure 5.14 Scatterplot of ln TV price and size of TV, with data-driven trend line

Table 5.11 Ln price of TV by independent variables. Bivariate regression (A) and multiple regression (B)

Independent variables	A	B
Size of TV (in inches)	0.057★★★ (0.002)	0.046★★★ (0.003)
Support 3D (no = 0; yes = 1)	–	0.494★★★ (0.062)
Constant	6.256	6.581
R^2	0.819	0.883
N	121	121

Note. Standard errors are in parentheses.

★ $p < 0.05$; ★★ $p < 0.01$; ★★★ $p < 0.001$ (two-tailed tests).

I said earlier that the regression coefficient expresses the change in y when x increases by one unit. When considering ln y, this changes. The general interpretation is now the change in y in *percent* when x increases by one unit. The coefficient in column A in Table 5.11 is 0.057. We multiple it by 100 to get the percentage:

5.7 percent. So, the difference in price between, say, a 54-inch TV and a 55-inch TV is 5.7 percent on average. (Yes, it is tempting to say that TV price increases with TV size, but TVs do not grow. We are comparing TVs of different sizes at one point in time.) The regression in column B contains an additional x-variable: the presence of 3D technology or not (no = 0; yes =1). Adjusted for the effect of this 3D variable, the regression coefficient for TV size is 0.046 or 4.6 percent.

You might be tempted to make the similar interpretation for the 3D coefficient: adjusted for the effect of TV size, a TV with 3D technology costs 49.4 percent more than a TV without this technology. Sorry, but that is a no-go. This "method" of interpretation is correct only for coefficients that fall within the approximate range of -0.15 to 0.15. For coefficients larger or smaller (as in more negative) than $-0.15/0.15$, we should use the following formula to get the correct percentage interpretation:

$$100 \times (e^b - 1).$$

Applying this to our example gives us $100 \times (2.71828^{0.494} - 1)$, which equals roughly 64 percent. So, adjusted for the effect TV size, a TV with 3D technology costs 64 percent more than a TV without this technology. (Technical note: $e^{0.494}$ means taking the antilogarithm of 0.494.)

Using ln y instead of y in a regression can often rectify the presence of minor non-linearities in the association between x and y. Plus, expressing interpretations in terms of percentages rather than numbers is often easier for many readers and other audiences to understand. Another benefit is that transforming a skewed variable by using logarithms often results in a more normally distributed variable, which can be preferable in certain situations. (More on the latter in Chapter 8.) For all these reasons, the ln y-regression — aka the semilogarithmic regression — has become the standard rather than the exception in regressions of prices, earnings, and expenditures. So, the next time you come across the phrase "the log of …" in a regression context, you will know that the regression coefficients in question typically refer to percentage differences in y.

KEY LEARNING POINTS

The key learning points in this chapter were:

- Multiple regression is an extension of bivariate regression allowing for several independent variables $(x_1, x_2, x_3, ...)$ to simultaneously affect.
- The technical interpretation of the multiple regression coefficient is the change in y given a one-unit increase in x_1, adjusted for the effect (or regression coefficient) of x_2 and x_3, and so on.
- Within the multiple regression framework, the typical interaction effect suggests that the magnitude of the regression coefficient of x_1 on y varies for different subgroups in the data.
- An interaction regression model includes an interaction term – a variable, say x_3 – that is the product of, say, variables x_1 and x_2.
- Multiple regression may be extended to handle both interaction effects and non-linear effects simultaneously.
- Multiple regression can handle situations in which the dependent variable, y, is a dummy. This is known as the LPM.
- Multiple *logistic* regression analysis is tailor-made for the situation in which y is a dummy, making sure that probabilities always fall between 0 and 100 percent.
- Using the natural logarithm of y, rather than the original y, in multiple regression might solve issues of non-linearity, non-normality, and practical difficulties in communicating regression results to larger audiences.

NOTES

1 In this example, the bivariate regression coefficient of x_1 (national team representation) was reduced in magnitude when x_2 (age of player) was added to the regression model. This is the typical case in real-life regressions. But it sometimes happens that x_1's regression coefficient *increases* in magnitude when x_2 is added to the regression model. This is known as a suppressor effect.

2 In other words, we are witnessing a suppressor effect (cf. endnote 1).

3 I emphasize again that there is no such thing as a high (as in good) or a low (as in bad) R^2. It all depends on the circumstances and on what has happened in earlier, related research.

4 In the technical sense, column A is a multiple regression. It includes three dummies, although it has only *one* independent variable: player position (having four categories).

5 I have discarded the 188 respondents having more than 12 doctor visits per year from the data. I'm *not* saying this is ok to do in general (see Chapter 8).

6 Several other requirements or assumptions must also be met if we are to trust the results of a regression analysis. I return to the explication of these regression assumptions in Chapter 8. See also the further reading section for introductions to the regression assumptions, and particularly Thrane (2022) for a non-technical account.

7 Non-linear and non-parallel regression lines are mathematical consequences of the inherent non-linearity of the logistic regression model. Consequently, they should not be interpreted as interaction effects and/or non-linear effects. Any such (potential) effects must be examined as shown previously in this chapter.

FURTHER READING

I recommend Thrane (2020, 2022), Berk (2004), Best and Wolf (2015), Gelman et al. (2021), and Allison (1999) as follow-ups to this chapter.

6

IDENTIFYING A CAUSAL EFFECT
Statistical and experimental control

DOI: 10.4324/9781032640808-6

INTRODUCTION

Despite using phrases like "x affects y" on several occasions in the book so far, we have only looked at statistical associations. This chapter takes a step back to scrutinize the nature of the associations in question. Are they merely statistical associations? Or do they reflect deeper, *causal* relationships? A causal relationship implies that it is the change in x_1, and not x_2, that prompts a change in y. When this happens, the phrase "x affects y" is justified in a cause-effect sense. We start by considering how multiple regression can be used as a tool to identify a causal relationship. In the lingo, this approach is known as the statistical control procedure. We then move on to the experimental control procedure. Finally, we use two new case studies to exemplify the experimental approach in a social science context.

STATISTICAL CONTROL: MULTIPLE REGRESSION, CONFOUNDING, AND SPURIOUSNESS

Our research question is to determine whether x_1 has a causal effect on y, not just to establish a statistical association between the two. In other words, we aim for making the giant leap from "x_1 is associated with y" to "x_1 affects y." Coming up is the way to proceed within a regression framework. First, we regress y on x_1 to see if there is a bivariate association to begin with. Second, we add other x-variables (x_2, x_3, x_4, ...) to the bivariate regression, making it a multiple regression. The idea is now that these other x-variables – *the control variables* – represent competing explanations for variation in y. Our interest lies in what happens to x_1's bivariate coefficient in the multiple regression.

We typically have three scenarios: (1) the size of x_1's coefficient, now a partial regression coefficient, is unaffected by the inclusion of the control variables. If this happens, we get support for interpreting x_1's effect as tentatively causal. (2) x_1's partial regression coefficient becomes nearly zero when the control variables are added to the regression. In this case, we get no support for interpreting x_1's effect as causal. (To clarify, a regression coefficient of zero suggests a horizontal regression line, implying no linear association between x_1 and y.) (3) x_1's partial regression coefficient gets reduced in magnitude but does not reach zero. Given that x_1 still has a substantively and statistically significant effect on y, we might — I emphasize *might* — interpret this as partial support for a causal effect. Yet this interpretation also requires certain other assumptions being met, but that is something for Chapter 8 and the further reading section.[1] One of our case studies will illustrate this reasoning in more detail.

CASE STUDY 3: THE PRICE, QUALITY RATING, AND ALCOHOL CONTENT OF BEERS, CONT.

Our research question is seemingly simple: does the quality of a beer have a causal effect on its price? Put differently, does a better tasting beer command a higher price? To explore this, column A in Table 6.1 shows a regression between beer price and taste quality. Remember that the Parker scale ranges from 50 points (undrinkable) to 100 points (perfect taste). The regression coefficient is NOK 4.37, and the regression line derived from this coefficient is shown in Figure 6.1: "Bivariate regression." The message is clear: beers with better taste seem to be more expensive; there is a bivariate effect to speak of. (Yes, a negative constant just implies that the regression line begins below zero on the y-axis.).

Now, the regression in column B controls for production country, making the quality effect a bit smaller in magnitude: NOK 3.88. The regression line from this adjusted coefficient also appears in Figure 6.1: "Adjusted for nationality." Controlling for production

Table 6.1 Beer bottle price by independent variables. Multiple linear regressions

Independent variables	A	B	C
Quality rating	4.37★★★ (0.74)	3.88★★★ (0.73)	1.70★ (0.66)
Production country (Sweden = 0, USA = 1)	–	27.56★★★ (5.24)	15.23★★ (4.70)
Alcohol content (in percent)	–	–	11.07★★★ (0.93)
Constant	−289.44	−266.34	−154.98
R^2	0.070	0.123	0.330
N	462	462	462

Note. Standard errors are in parentheses.

★ $p < 0.05$; ★★ $p < 0.01$; ★★★ $p < 0.001$ (two-tailed tests).

country does not alter our previous conclusion by much, though. Beers with better taste still seem to be more expensive. We are now talking about a result that aligns somewhat with scenario 1 mentioned above.

Moving on, column C controls for production country and alcohol content. We see that the quality effect now diminishes even further, going down from NOK 3.88 to just 1.70. The regression line resulting from this adjusted coefficient is also shown in Figure 6.1: "Adjusted for nationality and alcohol content." From a practical point of view, this regression line is almost horizontal. Our former conclusion – that beers with better taste seem to be more expensive – no longer applies in any real, substantive sense, even though the quality coefficient remains statistically significant. In terms of the three scenarios mentioned above, we are closer to scenario 2 than we are to scenario 3.

So, what is going on in the regression in column C? Why does the quality coefficient decrease so much when the alcohol content variable is added to the regression? It is time to introduce two key concepts in causal analysis: *confounding* and *spuriousness*. What we witnessed in Table 6.1 was a phenomenon called confounding; the

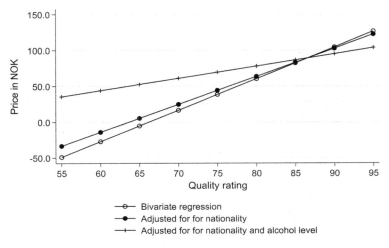

Figure 6.1 Three effects of taste quality on beer bottle price, based on the three regression models in Table 6.1

alcohol variable was a partial confounder of the bivariate association between quality and price. The reason for the drop in the size of the quality coefficient is depicted in Figure 6.2. Let's look at this figure in more detail.

Looking at column C in Table 6.1, we see that alcohol content affects price (coefficient = 11.07), as implied by the solid arrow between the two variables in Figure 6.2. We also note the weak effect of quality on price (coefficient = 1.70), as indicated by the dashed arrow. The new, intriguing element is the last vertical arrow: from alcohol content to taste quality. This arrow is the as-yet-undiscussed regression of quality on alcohol content, which yields a coefficient of 0.41 with a p-value less than 0.001 (not shown). This suggests that beers with higher alcohol content tend to receive better quality ratings than those with lower alcohol content.

So, what is the upshot of all this? Alcohol content acts as a confounder – a variable lurking in the background – explaining most of the bivariate association between quality and price. But since the initial bivariate association does not vanish altogether, as in becoming zero, the alcohol content variable is only a *partial* confounder.

The dashed arrow implies that the association between quality and price gets much weaker (but does not become zero) when the alcohol content variable is added the regression in column C in Table 6.1.

Earlier, we saw another example of partial confounding without mentioning it. When comparing the total number of matches

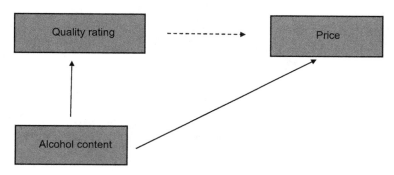

Figure 6.2 Alcohol content is a partial confounder of the association between quality and price

played for players with or without representation for their national teams, we found that the effect of the representation dummy became much smaller when adjusted for age; cf. column A versus column C in Table 5.1. More precisely, the coefficient for the representation dummy dropped from 95 to 28. Age was a partial confounder in this scenario; its inclusion in the regression model made the representation dummy's effect much smaller. But since the effect did not drop all the way down to zero, age was only a partial confounder.

The presence of confounding variables poses a fundamental threat to using multiple regression to identify causal effects. The problem is obvious when we start thinking about it. We can only adjust the effect of x_1 on y for the other x-variables included in our data. We cannot adjust/control/hold constant x-variables not included in our data. So, if we are to be certain that x_1 has this or that causal effect on y, we must make sure our data include all x-variables affecting y. This is a tall order, and most often it is too tall. Consider our beer data. What would happen to the quality variable's effect on price if some variable we do not have in our data, like the amount of wheat in the beers, is added to the regression in column C in Table 6.1? We do not know. It is possible that the quality variable's effect could become zero. And because we cannot rule this out for sure, we cannot trust the quality variable's effect to be causal. The conclusion is clear as day. Regression is not a bullet-proof causal analysis strategy whenever we are facing data like the ones we have analyzed in this book so far. For a more robust strategy, we need to look elsewhere but not necessarily far. The best strategy is to use an experimental research design, and this is something we'll dive into shortly.

But first, let's circle back to the topic of confounding. Suppose we found a bivariate association between x_1 and y, represented by a solid arrow between these variables. Suppose further that we then added the potential confounder, x_2, to the regression analysis, causing the bivariate association between x_1 and y to become zero. This, in essence, is the principle of *complete* confounding shown in Figure 6.3. The inclusion of x_2 makes the bivariate association between x_1 and y to totally disappear, essentially becoming zero. x_2 is therefore a total confounder. We might also say that x_2 in this case is the common cause of x_1 and y.

Spuriousness might be thought of as confounding's flipside. A spurious association implies a *false* or non-existing association. So,

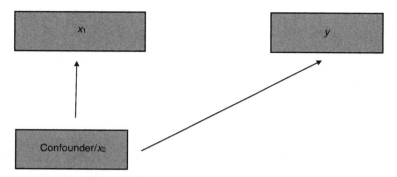

Figure 6.3 A confounder is a variable that totally explains the bivariate association between x_1 and y, as symbolized by the non-existent arrow between x_1 and y

whenever we find that some variable totally confounds the bivariate association between x_1 and y, this implies a spurious association between x_1 and y. In examples of partial confounding, in contrast, spuriousness is often expressed as a percentage. In our beer data, we could say that 61 percent of the quality variable's effect on price was spurious $((437-170)/437 = 0.61)$.

To accurately identify the causal effect of x_1 on y, we need to be 100 percent sure that we have ruled out the possibility of confounding. In this regard, it should be mentioned that there exist several more advanced and regression-based strategies that deal with confounding more effectively than the plain-vanilla regression model (see the further reading section). Still, none of these strategies are as effective as the experimental research design. A primer on identifying a causal effect by means of an experimental setup is coming up next.

EXPERIMENTAL CONTROL

It is hard, if not completely impossible, to watch a medical drama on TV without hearing about some "trial," which is shorthand for a randomized controlled trial (RCT). The RCT is essentially the mother of modern experimental designs. Here is how it works. People suffering from a specific disease, Y, are invited to participate in a trial. Let's say 50 patients meet the criteria to join, and that they get a box of pills with the instruction to take three a day for a two-week period. At the end of this period, all the patients (assuming no one drops out) undergo a diagnostic test for their disease. Let's say this test-variable, y, is measured on the scale from 0 (indicating no symptoms) to 10 (indicating severe symptoms). So far, so good, but this is still no experiment.

The crux of the matter happened behind the scenes in our fictitious trial, namely before the patients received their pill boxes. That is, there were two identical types of boxes save for one key difference: while half of the boxes contained pills with medicine, the other half contained placebo pills. (Medicine pills and placebo pills look and taste the same.) Also, and this is the crucial part, what dictated the decision to give a patient either medicine or placebo was a random mechanism akin to a coin toss (tails = placebo; heads = medicine). This so-called treatment decision is a dummy variable (placebo = 0; medicine = 1) in our vocabulary. With this in place, we have the plain-vanilla linear regression:

Diagnostic test or $y = b_0 + b_1 treatment$,

where b_1 or the regression coefficient is the average score difference on the diagnostic test between the patients receiving placebo (coded 0) and the patients receiving medicine (coded 1). Meanwhile, b_0 or the constant is the average score on this diagnostic test for the placebo group.

While the mechanics of the regression we are using here are nothing new, the interpretation of the results has a crucial twist. That is, we now interpret a negative and statistically significant regression coefficient/b_1 (a lower value on y indicates improvement) as the *causal* effect of the treatment on the disease. How come? The key lies in the treatment assignment procedure. Due to the randomness of the coin toss procedure, any association between the assignment dummy and other x-variables (such as genes, sex, age, dietary habits, fitness, health troubles, you name it) that could potentially explain improvement on the diagnostic test is purely coincidental. The random treatment assignment essentially solves any confounding problems before the study even begins, making other control variables superfluous given successful randomization. This, at its core, is what experimental control is all about.

The quest to identify causal effects is accelerating in the fast-paced world of modern research. With this as context, it is unsurprising that the RCT-logic just outlined has become increasingly popular in behavioral and social research in recent years. But let's not just talk about this – let's see it in action. Next up, we explore two new exemplary case studies from this setting.

DO WE TIP MORE IN RESTAURANTS WHEN OUR TABLE NEIGHBORS TIP MORE?

Imagine having enjoyed a nice restaurant meal with friends on a Saturday evening. For some reason you are expected to pay for your own meal, and soon it is your turn to pay the bill. When next in line you notice that the friend sitting next to you – who had the exact same meal as you – provides the waiter with a generous tip. Does witnessing your table neighbor's large tip influence the amount you are about to tip?

This research question is causal. The challenge in answering it lies in that the scenario only tells half the story. The other half, the potential scenario, is when your table neighbor provides a small tip or no tip at all. What would your tip amount have been then? More? Less? The same? The problem is that we do not get to "observe" both scenarios. We observe only one of them, just like a patient gets medicine or placebo – and not both. But in the restaurant setting we cannot randomly select our table neighbors' behavior by a coin toss. Or can we? Yes, we can – or at least sort of.

In a previous study, I described a scenario like the one above in a questionnaire.[2] The neighbor tip was NOK 60. I finished the scenario with the question, "How much do you tip?" But that was not the whole story, but only half of it. In the second version of the questionnaire, I described the similar scenario save for one feature: the neighbor tip was zero. Once again, I finished with the question, "How much do you tip?" In other words, the only difference between the questionnaires was the table neighbor's tip amount.

Now for the crucial idea. Before distributing the two types of questionnaires, I shuffled them all into a random pile of 500 questionnaires. This was my personal equivalent of a coin toss, ensuring that whatever scenario each respondent got was the result of a random mechanism. Long story short: I essentially mimicked an RCT within a restaurant tipping context.

In the restaurant tipping context, the random treatment variable is a dummy (no neighbor tip = 0; NOK 60 neighbor tip = 1). We then have our usual linear regression:

Tip amount or $y = b_0 + b_1$neighbor tip,

where b_1 or the regression coefficient is the average tip difference between the "diners" whose table neighbor provided no tip (coded 0) and the diners whose table neighbor provided a NOK 60 tip (coded 1). Meanwhile, b_0 or the constant is the average tip for the diners whose table neighbor provided no tip. The results of this experiment appear in column A in Table 6.2.

Column A tells a straightforward story. On average, diners seeing their table neighbor providing a NOK 60 tip gave a NOK 11 larger tip than diners seeing their table neighbor providing no tip. Also, the average tip for diners seeing their table neighbor giving no tip was almost NOK 20, as per the constant.[3]

In column B, the y-variable is the tip as a percentage of the total bill. On average, diners seeing their table neighbor providing a NOK 60 tip gave a 2.7 percentage points larger tip than diners seeing their table neighbor providing no tip. The average tip percentage for diners seeing their table neighbor giving no tip was 5 percent (the constant).[4] Lastly, column C is a LPM distinguishing between diners providing a tip (coded 1) and diners not providing a tip (coded 0).

Table 6.2 Three aspects of tipping by table neighbor's tipping behavior. Bivariate linear regressions

Independent variables	A	B	C
	Tip amount	Tip percent	Tip probability
Table neighbor's tip (no tip = 0; NOK 60 tip = 1)	11.273★★★ (2.094)	0.027★★★ (0.005)	0.145★★ (0.042)
Constant	19.648	0.050	0.600
R^2	0.056	0.052	0.024
N	489	489	489

Note. Standard errors are in parentheses.

★ $p < 0.05$; ★★ $p < 0.01$; ★★★ $p < 0.001$ (two–tailed tests).

On average, diners seeing their table neighbor providing a NOK 60 tip had an almost 15 percentage points higher probability of providing a tip than diners seeing their table neighbor providing no tip.

The answer to the research question serving as this section's heading – do we tip more in restaurants when our table neighbors tip more? – is easy to sum up. Yes, our neighbors' tipping behavior affect our own tipping behavior. And since we can rule out any confounding effects by our research design (i.e., by experimental control), the effect in question is causal. Still, it is important to note that the size of the causal effect applies to the entire sample as an average effect. There might be interaction effects that should be scrutinized along the lines we saw in Chapter 5. (More on this shortly.)

We had only one experimental dummy in the exemplary case study above. We might also have two or more such experimental dummies. With that in mind, now for a second experiment of mine from the wining and dining business.[5]

ARE CONSUMERS AFFECTED BY EXPERTS' QUALITY SCORES AND PEER RECOMMENDATIONS WHEN BUYING WINE?

As mentioned earlier, Norwegians must buy alcoholic beverages with a higher alcohol content than 4.75 percent in state-run outlets called Vinmonopolet. In a previous study, I described a scenario like the following to the respondents: "You are at Vinmonopolet, looking through the shelves. A wine you have heard of but not tasted catches your interest." The respondents then got a set of questions based on a random procedure. One group was told the wine had mainly gotten quality scores of 5 points by experts (a very good wine) *and* that a knowledgeable peer had recommended it. A second group received the same quality information but no peer recommendation cue. A third group was told the wine had mainly gotten quality scores of 3 points by experts (an ok wine) *and* a peer recommendation cue, while a fourth group received the same quality information but no peer recommendation. Finally, all respondents got the same question, "On a scale from 1 (not likely) to 9 (very likely), how likely is it that you will buy the wine in question if it is white and costs 150 NOK?"

In this exemplary case study, we have two experimental dummies: wine experts' quality scores (3 or 5 points) and peer recommendation (no or yes). Column A in Table 6.3 shows how these two dummies affect the probability of buying a white wine. The results are easy to summarize. Adjusted for the effect of peer recommendation, a wine obtaining 5 quality points has a 1.77-point larger buying probability than a wine obtaining 3 quality points (on a 10-point scale). Similarly, adjusted for the effect of quality, a peer-recommended wine has a 0.55-point larger buying probability than a wine with no such recommendation. The difference in magnitude between these two regression coefficients is also evident, and it suggests that favorable expert reviews pack a much bigger punch than peer recommendations when it comes to the influence on buying white wine.[6] In any event, we can still answer the research question posed as this section's heading – are consumers affected by experts' quality scores and peer recommendations when buying wine? – in the affirmative.

Column B in Table 6.3 scrutinizes a possible interaction effect between the two experimental dummies. We find a negative and statistically significant interaction effect, which also is shown in Figure 6.4. The figure reveals that peer recommendations only seem to apply to wines obtaining quality scores of 3 points (ok wines), and not to wines obtaining quality scores of 5 points (very good wines). Put bluntly, when it comes to wines, consumers do not need peer advice when buying products that experts already have assessed as very good.[7]

Table 6.3 Buying probability of white wine by quality score and peer recommendation. Multiple linear regressions

Independent variables	A	B
Quality score (3 points = 0, 5 points = 1)	1.774★★★ (0.229)	2.361★★★ (0.294)
Peer recommendation (no = 0; yes = 1)	0.553★ (0.228)	1.430★★★ (0.360)
Quality score × peer recommendation	–	−1.448★★ (0.462)
Constant	4.796	4.453
R²	0.133	0.152
N	441	441

Note. Standard errors are in parentheses.

★ $p < 0.05$; ★★ $p < 0.01$; ★★★ $p < 0.001$ (two-tailed tests).

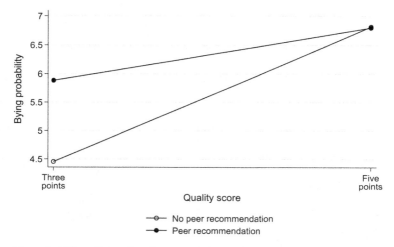

Figure 6.4 The effects of quality score points and peer recommendation on the probability of buying white wine, based on the regression model in column B in Table 6.3

IDENTIFYING CAUSAL EFFECTS IN THE SOCIAL AND BEHAVIORAL SCIENCES

For anyone aiming to identify a causal relationship, the experimental design or RCT is the natural place to start. That said, experiments or RCTs are for several reasons not always feasible to conduct in the social and behavioral sciences – be they practical, financial, or ethical.[8] The two preceding sections have also shown that regression analysis might be used as a tool for doing causal analysis.

This makes the adage "correlation does not imply causation" somewhat of a misnomer, considering that regression is a form of correlational analysis. What this adage means, or *should* refer to, is the caveat that observational data (to which correlation or regression is typically applied) are never ideal for making causal claims. For experimental data, in contrast, regression works fine as an identifier of causal effects. As someone humorously noted on Facebook the other day, "Everyone that confuses correlation and causation eventually ends up dead."

KEY LEARNING POINTS

The key learning points in this chapter were:

- Multiple regression analysis on observational data might put us on the trace of a causal effect. But it cannot prove causation with any confidence.
- The (potential) problems of confounding and spuriousness always plague multiple regression models carried out on observational data.
- Proving that x_1 has a causal effect on y with any confidence requires some type of experimental design.
- The so-called RCT is the most effective way of identifying a causal effect.
- RCTs/experimental designs have become more popular in the social and behavioral sciences of late.
- Interaction effects must be examined in experimental/RCT designs in the same way they are scrutinized for observational data.
- Regression analysis might be used to identify a causal effect within the context of RCTs or other experimental design.

NOTES

1 For example, we must make sure x_1 precedes y in time to avoid *reverse* causality. This is difficult to achieve for questionnaire-type data. We must also make sure that the multiple regression controls for all relevant x-variables, which the main text and Chapter 8 says more about later. If not, we get omitted variable bias (see Chapter 8 and the further reading section).

2 Thrane and Haugom (2020) provide more background.

3 Recall from Chapter 2 that tipping is not mandatory in Norway, explaining the small tip amounts provided.

4 R^2 typically plays little role in regression-based experimental studies.

5 Thrane (2019) offers for more background. These data were also mentioned in Chapter 2 (cf. endnote 5), and they refer to a so-called *survey experiment*.

6 By means of a significance test, we can also examine whether the effect of the expert review dummy is *larger* than the effect of the peer recommendation dummy. Drum roll ... It is significantly larger ($p = 0.0002$).

7 In practice, we often supplement studies like these with the use of some key control variables. For example, it might be that the random assignment procedure did not work out as well as it should have. When this happens, control variables could become relevant.

8 Many considerations limit our research design choices in the social and behavioral sciences. For example, we cannot in all good conscience place people in potentially jeopardizing situations (serving as either treatment or placebo) purely for the sake of determining the causal effect of x_1 on y. In most cases, the ends simply do *not* justify the means.

FURTHER READING

I recommend Cunningham (2021), Huntington-Klein (2022), Best and Wolf (2015), Pearl and Mackenzie (2018), and Rosenbaum (2017) as follow-ups to this chapter.

7

STATISTICAL ANALYSIS IN PRESENT-DAY LIFE

CHAPTER OVERVIEW

DOI: 10.4324/9781032640808-7

INTRODUCTION

Statistical research can be tricky, and things sometimes go awry. A common denominator in this chapter is the evaluation of statistical research. We'll start with data collection and then move on to data analysis, before taking on the interpretation and communication of results. Next, we'll address some problems in the current practice of significance testing, followed by three sections showcasing the formerly discussed topics using our familiar case study data sets. The last two sections bring up some critical issues regarding how statistical research typically is presented to us in the news.[1]

At the end of the day, statistical *results* are based on analyses of data someone has put in rows and columns in a spreadsheet-like matrix. Two issues are critical inputs here: data *collection* and data *analysis*. The upcoming section covers the former, the next one addresses the latter.

DATA COLLECTION: PITFALLS AND PROBLEMS

"Garbage in, garbage out" is an old saying relevant for data collection. It suggests, obviously, that no amount of well-thought data analysis can save faulty data from bringing about wrongful conclusions. Popular science books are packed with illustrating stories, and one of the most (in)famous concerns the two economists Reinhart and Rogoff. In 2010, they published a paper showing, for a sample of countries, an association between some x and some y. This association was then used by politicians to justify changes in public policy. In 2013, however, critics found out that some countries – due to a typo in Reinhart and Rogoff's spreadsheet! – were missing in the regression model yielding the association between x and y. And when these missing countries were included in the sample (as they should), the association between x and y became much weaker than the one Reinhart and Rogoff reported in their original 2010 paper.[2] To drive the point all the way home: "garbage in, garbage out."

Reinhart and Rogoff's mistake was a mere typo – or, at worst, negligence. And we can only speculate on the extent to which such typos cause erroneous conclusions in present-day statistical results. (My personal take is that such typos appear in abundance, but let's not get into that.) The more extreme version of "bad data collection" is when researchers make up – as in fabricate – the numbers in their spreadsheets. Why would they do that? The simple reason is that manipulated data always give the researchers the conclusion they want ... Ironically, a recent infamous story concerns, of all things, a research project on people's *honesty*.[3]

A researcher had this idea that people might be more honest in their answers if they sign an honesty pledge at the beginning of an application rather than at the end, as in after they have answered the questions. This seems entirely reasonable on the face of it. To test this hypothesis in a car insurance setting, the researcher randomly distributed two types of applications – one with the honesty pledge at the beginning of the application, and one with the pledge at the end – to prospective car insurance customers. This was the treatment dummy, x_1, in our vocabulary. The y-variable was, to simplify a bit, the amount of cheating in the answers given. The result? The study revealed, rather unsurprisingly, that cheating was about 10 percent *lower* among the customers who received the honesty pledge at the beginning of the application. The hypothesis, it seemed, was supported – so far, so good.

Fast-forward a few years. Some other researchers managed to get hold of a copy of the spreadsheet containing the original data for the study. Through some detective-work they made, much to their surprise, a startling discovery. Some of the answers given by the signing-at-the-start group had been transferred to the signing-at-the-end group and vice versa – to produce the results suggested by the hypothesis and reported in the study. But when these answers were transferred back to their original place in the spreadsheet, the statistical analysis revealed a very different story: cheating was more prevalent among the signing-at-the-start group.

The car insurance study serves as a disheartening but illustrative example of how researchers (might) fabricate data to get the results they want. (Disclaimer: the final chapter on this scandal has probably not been written yet, but that does not diminish the general point being made here).[4] The important matter at stake concerns the multitude of other instances of data fabrication having gone under the radar over the years. We do not know how many there are. But to say "lots of" them probably falls very short of the grim reality.

Now, let's pivot to something completely different. The discus throw is a track and field sports event. A sports researcher slash inventor has come up with a new technique for throwing the discus, with the promise that it will enable athletes to throw longer. To test this (yes, that is a research question), he has invited the 47 best Norwegian discus throwers to participate in a study. While one random half of the throwers took a two-hour course to learn the new technique, the other half was told to stay put, warm up, and throw the discus using their normal routine. The researcher then arranged a competition. The best result out of three attempts (measured in

Table 7.1 Test results for discus throws measured in meters. Underlined numbers are for athletes using the new throwing technique

Athlete number	Meters	Athlete number	Meters
1	65.82	25	61.85
2	49.42	26	63.33
3	52.16	27	57.02
4	59.12	28	64.92
5	69.24	29	52.62
6	71.95	30	70.82
7	67.15	31	68.16
8	66.38	32	68.55
9	51.63	33	65.05
10	59.72	34	49.00
11	56.57	35	55.22
12	70.96	36	54.92
13	64.34	37	69.67
14	68.62	38	66.97
15	58.77	39	70.34
16	67.02	40	67.18
17	63.91	41	68.99
18	70.13	42	70.22
19	55.52	43	62.52
20	62.15	44	65.15
21	64.63	45	68.36
22	71.45	46	65.75
23	66.18	47	62.05
24	59.62		

Note. 70 meters ≈ 2,756 inches or 76.55 yards.

meters) is shown for each athlete in Table 7.1, where the underlined numbers represent the throws with the new technique.

By coding the traditional technique as 0 and the new technique as 1, we may think of the present competition data along our previous regression-based experiments, as in:

Discus throw in meters = $b_0 + b_1$ technique,

where b_1 or the regression coefficient is the average difference in throwing length between the athletes using the traditional technique (coded 0) and the athletes using the new technique (coded 1). Meanwhile, b_0 or the constant is the average throw length in meters for the athletes using the traditional technique. The results appear in Table 7.2.

Table 7.2 tells a simple story. On average, the athletes using the new technique threw 4.22 meters longer than the athletes sticking with the traditional technique. The latter threw 61.27 meters on average, as per the constant. The difference between the two groups is statistically significant at the 5 percent level. So, much to the relief of the researcher slash inventor, we conclude that the new discus throw technique seems to outperform the old one. But is that the whole story?

Let's take closer look at the last digit in each of the 47 results listed in Table 7.1. (Keep in mind, the two last digits refer to centimeters.) For the first and second throws, the number is 2. For the third throw, it is 6. Nothing unusual so far. But if you sift through all the numbers, a pattern begins to emerge. Some numbers, like 2 and 5, show up quite often, while others, such as 0, 1, and 9, are rare.

Table 7.2 Discus throw in meters by technique based on the data in Table 7.1. Linear regression

Independent variables	
Technique (traditional = 0; new = 1)	4.22 (1.75)★
Constant	61.27
R^2	0.114
N	47

Note. Standard errors are in parentheses.

★ $p < 0.05$ (two-tailed test).

Considering that each number from 0 to 9 should have an equal probability of showing up in a long series of throws, how likely is the pattern in Table 7.1? The answer is not likely, or 0.04 percent likely. These data have probably been fabricated to ensure that the researcher got the results he wanted. I can even be more certain here. I *know* these data have been fabricated because I made them up.[5]

Regardless of its content, the silver lining in this story is the reminder that careful inspection can sometimes expose fraudulent data. Data showing too little variation or too little randomness are typical telltales of made-up data. For example, many people have a tendency of overreporting the number 7 when asked do come up with some "random" number.[6] So, lots of 7-ens in a spreadsheet are suspicious! You should also be skeptical when you come across a large random sample of infants with a 60:40 sex ratio. No, this does not happen in real life. The not-so-positive implication of this story concerns what we do not get to see. In most cases, the audience – you, me, and other researchers – do not get to inspect the data a study is based on because of authors' data ownership.[7] Well, so much for data collection – bogus or not. Now, let's turn our attention to data analysis and interpretation of results.

DATA ANALYSIS AND INTERPRETATION OF RESULTS: A LONG AND WINDING ROAD

For the sake of the argument, let's assume that the data collection has gone without a glitch and that the data by all accounts are beyond reproach. What remains are the analyses and the interpretations of the results of these analyses. What can possibly go wrong at this stage? The answer is a whole lot, even though the first six chapters of this book hopefully will help you spot or avoid many common mistakes. As for the analysis part, one problem has to do with the correct way of analyzing the data. Or, more accurately, with the fact that there often is not one correct way of analyzing the data. Also, slightly different statistical techniques might yield very different results. When conducting your own research, you have some measure of control over this. When considering research done by others, however, you only get to see the results that somehow "survived" the data analysis process. But these surviving results are for several reasons not necessarily correct.[8]

I previously mentioned that we rarely get access to the original data used in a study. A related issue is that we in most cases neither get to know what happened during the *exploratory* phase of the data analysis. What we do get to know in abundance, though, are the result of statistical analyses – such as the regression equation. Suppose the following plain-vanilla regression result was presented to you in a study:

$$y = 3.0 + 0.5x,$$

suggesting the familiar and upward sloping regression line, with a regression coefficient of 0.5 and a constant of 3.0. At first glance it would seem reasonable to suggest the interpretation that x (which could be anything) has a positive effect on y (which could also be anything) if the 0.5 coefficient has a p-value at 5 percent or below. Scenario A in Figure 7.1 is the visual version of the regression just mentioned. The data points are scattered around the regression line just as one would expect. In short, everything seems to be in order – at least for the time being. Yet this conclusion is very premature.

Scenario B shows us why this conclusion is the premature. The regression line in scenario B has the same regression coefficient (0.5) and constant (3.0) as in scenario A. In other words, the obvious *non-linear* association between x and y in scenario B yields the exact same (aggregated) regression results as scenario A. The takeaway? Since we most often in studies only get to see the "final" regression models, and not the exploratory scatterplots, we are left to trust that researchers have performed the required legwork before publishing their results. The old saying "trust but verify" seems particularly apt in this context, at least seen from where I'm standing.

Scenarios C and D are two more examples of data patterns yielding the same aggregated regression results: regression coefficient = 0.5 and constant = 3.0. In both scenarios, one outlier brings about the results. So much for data analysis at this point, let's turn to the interpretation of statistical results.

Interpreting statistical results correctly presents its own set of challenges. If you are in charge of data collection and analysis, you can "control the story" as to how results are to be interpreted and

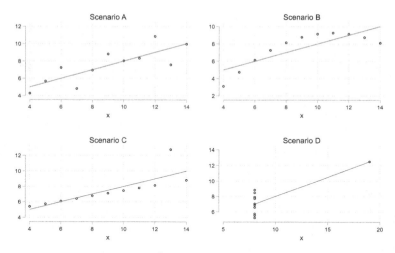

Figure 7.1 Anscombe's quartet[9]

communicated. When other peoples' research is at stake, however, the interpretation of results often shows up in one of two guises: those made by researchers themselves, or those made by journalists reporting on research carried out by others. To be frank, both might be flawed but the latter tends to be more prone to errors. The difference between relative and absolute risk is a classic. Here we go, or should I say run?

Imagine a team of sports researchers who have been tracking thousands of runners in a multi-year project. One study emerging from this project yielded the results reported in Table 7.3. (Yes, this is a mock study, but it is filled with all the correct and tasty ingredients. You can also assume that the study includes many control variables, and that it ticks all boxes from a technical standpoint.)

Table 7.3 shows that the probability of having a heart fibrillation problem is 2 percent among those who eat carrots. And among those who do not eat carrots, the similar figure is 3 percent. The ratio of these numbers, the *risk ratio*, comes out at 2/3 or 0.67: carrot eaters have a 33 percent lower risk of having a heart fibrillation problem than those not eating carrots (100−67 = 33). This 33 percent group difference, typically highlighted in media outlets, sounds massive. A 33 percent less chance of heart fibrillation? Time

Table 7.3 Results from a study on the association between carrot eating and heart fibrillation

	Has heart fibrillation	*No heart fibrillation*
Not eaten carrots	3%	97%
Eaten carrots	2%	98%

to stock up on those carrots! But something still does not feel right here. The relative risk difference overshadows the absolute risk difference, which in this case is only 1 percentage point (98−97 = 1). And when we take this absolute risk difference into account, as we should, there are few compelling reasons to start eating carrots (unless you particularly enjoy their taste). In essence, absolute risk differences are often more crucial than relative risk differences from a policy perspective, although the latter get most of the press attention.[10] There are countless other examples of imprecise or misleading research communication. A thorough discussion of how to communicate research results accurately and effectively is beyond the scope of this book, though.

Let's change the subject − in a *significant* manner, I should perhaps add.

INFERENCES AND NHST: SIGNIFICANCE TESTING GONE WILD

Suppose your data is a random sample from a large, unknown population. The question of statistical inference then boils down to whether it is ok to claim that your sample finding − typically a statistical association of some kind − also applies to the broader population in question. Once more, it is time to meet the Holy Grail of statistical research: the Null Hypothesis Significance Test procedure or NHST. The NHST procedure has been criticized almost since its inception. But in recent years, this critique has become much more vocal. Below follows some key points.

Chapter 4 said that a *p*-value of 5 percent or lower suggested some kind of systematic association between *x* and *y* being present in the population of interest. This does not mean, as many seem to think, that *x* has a strong or important effect on *y*. Rather, it just suggests that the effect in question is likely larger than zero in the population. There is, in short, a fundamental difference between being statistically significant on the one hand and being practically or economically significant on the other hand.

The issue of practical versus statistical significance also concerns sample size. As we saw in Chapter 4, the standard error "automatically" got smaller in larger samples, all else being equal. It follows from this that tiny associations, or very small group differences, become statistically significant at the 5 percent level in large samples. The implication of this, for moderately large to large samples at least, is that a p-value below 5 percent for a statistical association is even less of an importance signal than it would be in small or medium-sized samples.

Sometimes we do not get what we want. Let's say our 0.5 regression coefficient mentioned some paragraphs back was statistically significant at $p = 0.03$. We hope the similar but unknown coefficient in the population is close to 0.5. But the p-value of 0.03 does not tell us much about the probability of the sample regression coefficient mirroring the size of the regression coefficient in the unknown population. We want a high probability of the coefficient being close to 0.5 in the population. What we get instead is a 3 percent (0.03) probability of finding a coefficient of 0.5 in our sample, or a larger one, assuming the true coefficient in the unknown population is zero. Talk about getting a different kettle of fish!

Another problem with the NHST procedure has to do with the nature of the null hypothesis. Suppose prior research has consistently yielded regression coefficients of around 0.4 for the association between x and y. Now, suppose that the x-y coefficient in your sample is 0.5. You probably see where I'm going with this. Why should we compare a coefficient of 0.5 with a coefficient of 0.0 when we have reason to believe a more suitable comparison yardstick would be 0.4? The NHST procedure has little to offer here. (Apologies again.)

Finally, what is so special about the threshold of $p = 0.050$? Why not 0.040 or 0.060? And why should we believe in an x-y association in the population when $p = 0.050$ but reject such an association when $p = 0.051$? There are two points to be made here. First, the 0.050 threshold is a convention roughly corresponding to 95 out of 100 correct inferences in the long run (or the t-value of ± 1.96).

Second, and more importantly, we should not get caught up in this dual kind of thinking in the first place. Rather, we should focus on the magnitude of, say, the regression coefficient and acknowledge that practical significance trumps statistical significance six ways to Sunday.

Given the above problems, and some others I cannot get into for the sake of page space, it is not surprising that many researchers have recommended that the whole NHST-enchilada should be abandoned. This raises a new question: if not NHST, then what should we use to evaluate sample associations when it comes to making inferences about the population in question? Two key words that might provide a good start in this regard are confidence intervals (CIs) and effect sizes.

The practice of reporting CI in addition to the so-called point estimates (e.g., regression coefficients, differences between means or fractions) has long been considered prudent in statistical research. The more recent suggestion is to make such reporting mandatory, and not only advisable. This implies that when we report, say, a sample regression coefficient, we should also report its CI to inform our readers that the *real* (but unknown) coefficient in the population might be much larger or smaller than our sample coefficient. Mandatory reporting of effect sizes has been proposed in the same vein. Effect-size measures are handy rule-of-thumb guides for classifying variable associations as small, medium, or large. Now, let's look at some CIs and effect sizes by returning to some of our case studies.

CASE STUDY 4: THE WELL-BEING OF NORWEGIANS, CONT.

By means of a bivariate regression, Table 3.4 reported an association between subjective well-being and the presence of any long-lasting illnesses or health problems. Table 7.4 recasts this association in terms of an ANOVA (analysis of variance). We note that the non-problem group, on average, reports 0.805-points higher subjective well-being than the problem group: $8.421 - 0.805 = 7.616$. (Yes, this difference is the regression coefficient of -0.81 in Table 3.4.) Furthermore, the association is statistically significant, with a very low p-value.

Table 7.4 Subjective well-being by presence of long-lasting illnesses or health problems. ANOVA. N = 6,539

	Mean	N
Presence of long-lasting illnesses or health problems		
No	8.421 (1.426)	4,035
Yes	7.616 (1.889)	2,504
Mean difference	0.805	

Note. Standard deviations are in parentheses. The mean difference has a p-value of < 0.00001.

Table 7.5 Subjective well-being by presence of long-lasting illnesses or health problems. ANOVA. 95 percent CI and Cohen's d. N = 6,539.

	Mean	N
Presence of long-lasting illnesses or health problems		
No	8.421 (1.426)	4,035
Yes	7.616 (1.889)	2,504
Mean difference/95 percent CI	0.805/[0.724, 0.885]	
Cohen's d	0.499	

Note. Standard deviations are in parentheses. The mean difference has a p-value of < 0.00001.

Table 7.4 reveals the problem with the NHST procedure: we do not get to know the probable size of the group difference in the population, nor do we get to know if this difference should be regarded as small, medium, or large. Table 7.5 includes the necessary amendments to answers these questions as well.

To simplify a great deal, the CI suggests that the group difference in subjective well-being in the population likely falls between 0.72 and 0.89.[11] Cohen's d is 0.50, suggesting that the 0.805-points group difference might be regarded as a medium-sized effect. As general rules-of-thumb, a Cohen's d of 0.20 (or −0.20) is a small effect, and a Cohen's d of 0.80 (or −0.80) is a large effect. The contents of Table 7.5 might alternatively be presented in a graph, like in Figure 7.2.

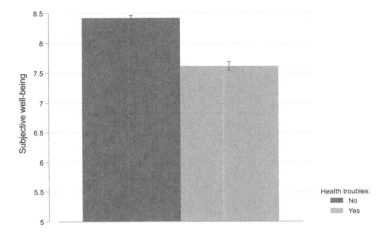

Figure 7.2 Subjective well-being by presence of long-lasting illnesses or health problems (no or yes), with 95 percent CIs. Graph based on the results of Table 7.5

CASE STUDY 1: THE TYPICAL QUANTITATIVE CHARACTERISTICS OF PIZZA RESTAURANT MEALS, CONT.

Let's return to our restaurant data and to the association between the total bill for the meal and the number of diners taking part in it. Table 7.6 supplements the results shown in Table 3.2 with some new information on a significance test and a CI.

As expected, the regression coefficient in Table 7.6 is statistically significant, with its 95 percent CI ranging from NOK 106 to NOK 144. The question of whether this NOK 125 coefficient should be deemed as small, medium, or large can be evaluated against the size of the correlation coefficient (cf. Chapter 3). In this example, the regression coefficient of 125 corresponds to a correlation coefficient of 0.60. In general, a correlation coefficient of 0.20 (or −0.20) suggests a small effect, while a correlation of 0.80 (or −.080) suggests a large effect. Lastly, a correlation coefficient of 0.50 (or −0.50) implies a medium-sized effect. The effect of number of diners can, in other words, be considered between medium and large. We may also display the 95 percent CI for the regression coefficient of the number of diners variable in a graph. Figure 7.3 takes care of this.[12]

Table 7.6 Total bill for meal by number of diners. Linear regression

Independent variable	B	95 percent CI
Number of diners	125 (9.6)★★★	[106, 144]
Constant	211	
R^2	0.36	
N	300	

Note. Standard errors are in parentheses.
★★★ $p < 0.01$ (two-tailed test).

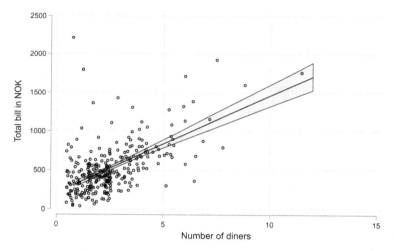

Figure 7.3 Total bill for meal by number of diners, with 95 percent CI. Graph based on the results of Table 7.6

Questions regarding CIs and effect sizes are common in regression and ANOVA settings. But such effect sizes might also be relevant for cross-tabulations, as the next example from our football data shows.

EFFECT SIZES FOR CROSS-TABULATIONS

Table 3.5 presented the association between national team representation and player nationality. This table re-appears in Table 7.7, where I also have added some new information. Fourteen percent

Table 7.7 National team representation by nationality. Cross-tabulation. Percentages

National team representation	Nationality		
	Norwegian	*Foreign*	*Total*
No	86	70	81
Yes	14	30	19
Total	100 (214)	100 (96)	100 (310)
Cohen's *w*	0.198		

Note. Numbers in parentheses are actual frequencies. Pearson chi-square $(1, n = 310)$ $= 12.09, p = 0.001$.

of the Norwegian players have represented national teams, whereas the similar percentage for the foreign players is 30 percent. The effect-size question is about assessing this 16-percentage points difference $(30 - 14 = 16)$, which in practice boils down to calculating Cohen's *w*. A Cohen's *w* of 0.10 implies a small effect, whereas 0.30 is a medium effect. Lastly, 0.50 is considered a large effect. Our present effect lands somewhere between small and medium-sized.[13]

BIASED SAMPLES, BIASED CONCLUSIONS

Biased samples threaten research conclusions in many more ways than we like to think of. While such biased samples may take on many forms, they tend to have one thing in common: they have *not* been generated by a random selection procedure.[14] Among these "convenience samples" (for want of a better word), two types of samples stand out as especially relevant: *selected* samples and *self-selected* samples. (The latter is a special case of the former.)

A selected sample means that a unit, say a person, must satisfy some criteria to become part of the sample. Keeping the scenario, a self-selected sample implies that it is the person who decides to satisfy the criteria or not. To clarify, when we studied wine club members in Chapter 2, we studied a self-selected sample: these members had at some earlier point in time themselves decided to join a wine club (the self-selection criteria). Conversely, when studying a sample of convicted felons, we are dealing with a selected sample: these felons have all committed some crime at some earlier point in time (the selection criteria). Both types of samples can be potentially problematic in terms of yielding biased results. Sometimes this is obvious, as the next example illustrates. In others, it is not so clear-cut – as we also shall see.

Table 2.3 presented the agreements with the statement "I often discuss wine with my family, friends, and colleagues" among 468 Norwegian wine club members. About one-third of the members totally agreed with this statement. Now, imagine this statement being presented to a random sample of the Norwegian adult population. What would the similar percentage be? We do not know, obviously, but we have every reason to believe that it would be much smaller than one-third. The reason is clear as day. A more-than-average wine interest is what makes people join a wine club. This interest, in turn, creates a self-selected sample with a more-than-average wine interest. The kicker is that we should always exercise caution when making inferences from (self-)selected samples to broader populations.

A more subtle problem arises when associating the wine statement variable with another x-variable, for example biological sex as in Table 3.10. Here, we found that male members were more likely to totally agree with the statement than female members, the difference being 17 percentage points. Is it safe to assume that this sex difference would be of the same size if the data were a random sample of the Norwegian population. The answer is probably not, to err on the side of caution. Such a comparison could reveal a smaller or a larger sex difference – or it could flip the script entirely by showing that women were more in agreement with the statement than men. The overarching message is that we should also be cautious when making inferences about variable associations to general populations based on analyses of (self-)selected samples.

A famous "study" of a selected sample concerns the so-called 10,000-hour rule.[15] Based on data from many top-notch athletes, Malcolm Gladwell found an association between preparation and super-success: practice for 10,000 hours! In other words, practice for 10,000 hours and you can accomplish anything. The problem with this reasoning is that it is, well, utterly wrong. And you understand why. Gladwell is studying a selected sample: those having a tremendous amount of success. He does not study all the other athletes, surely outnumbering those having great success, who did *not* make it to the top. And herein lies the rub. If we want to identify the association (by a regression analysis, say) between preparation and success, we must study the ones having success as well as the ones not having such success. Again, making inferences based on biased samples can be a risky or dangerous sport. (Or game, if you prefer.)

ASKING CRITICAL QUESTIONS ABOUT STATISTICAL RESEARCH: DEVELOPING A BULLSHIT DETECTOR

There is always the possibility of a bullshit story whenever you come across a statistical study reported in some media outlet.[16] In this section, I'm going to highlight some useful considerations and questions to keep in mind when evaluating statistical research as it is typically presented to us in the news.

One of the most crucial questions in statistical research concerns the adage of correlation versus causation. Does a study make a causal claim about a cause-and-effect relationship, or is it just about a statistical association? Let's say the researchers have causal aspirations; they maintain to have established that x causes y in the manner that some medication cures some disease. An immediate question then pops up: did the researchers use an RCT or something similar to identify the purported causal effect?[17] If the answer is yes, we might relax a bit — at least temporarily (cf. Chapter 6). But if the answer is no, a series of questions emerges: what kind of data are we talking about? Cross-sectional, longitudinal, or both?[18] Where the data collected by the researchers specifically for the research question at hand, or did they use data collected by others. Did the data collection involve a random selection procedure, or are we talking about a convenience sample or some other selected sample? The general answer is that longitudinal data collected by a random mechanism and tailor-made to the specific research question are better than the other alternatives mentioned for making *tentative* causal claims (cf. Chapters 5 and 6). At the other end of the scale of preference, we have the selected or one-shot convenience samples. Such data are in general never suitable for making anything remotely close to causal claims.

So, the first question you should ask when coming across some study relating this x with that y should be: does the study have casual aspirations? If the answer is yes, proceed down the path of the questions just posed. Furthermore, and assuming everything checks out so far, you might find it helpful to consider a few more questions[19]:

- Who is behind the research? Do they have any financial or other (prestigious) stakes in the research project?

Obviously, research findings from bodies deeply invested into the project – in every sense of this economic term – warrant more scrutiny than otherwise equal or similar research. Enough said about that.

- Besides being statistically significant, is the causal effect practically significant? What is the effect size? Is the sample size so large that any statistical association, no matter how minor and trivial, is statistically significant?[20] Does it make theoretical and/ or practical sense for x to influence y in the manner prescribed by the researchers? Further comments are superfluous.
- Has the reported research undergone a robust quality-checking procedure?

These days, quality-checking amounts to research being published in scientific journals of high standard. That said, the distinction between a high-standard journal and a not-so-high-standard journal can often be blurry and is hotly debated. Still, PowerPoint presentations downloaded from the Internet are not necessarily quality-checked research.

Lastly, we have the fundamental bullshit detector question:

- Does the research finding seem *too* good to be true?

If it does, it probably is.

After reading this book, I hope you have developed something of a keen bullshit detector for spotting questionable, or in a few cases (?), outright bad statistical research practices.

KEY LEARNING POINTS

The key learning points in this chapter were:

- The quality of the incoming data puts severe restrictions on the quality of the outgoing statistical conclusions: "garbage in, garbage out."
- Statistical textbooks and "common statistical sense" (for lack of a better term) do not always offer clear-cut answers to what the correct data analysis for the research question at hand is – or should be. Much can thus go wrong in data analyses, and the subsequent results might be flawed.
- Both researchers and journalists sometimes make imprecise or flat-out wrongful interpretations of statistical results.
- The Null Hypothesis Inference-regime – the NHST procedures – is marred with problems.
- Reporting CIs and effect sizes represent improvements to the traditional NHST-regime.
- Biased samples sometimes place severe restrictions on the possibilities of valid generalizations to broader populations.
- When coming across new and/or sensational statistical research findings, it might be wise to scrutinize the claims made by using, well, a bullshit detector.

NOTES

1 This chapter draws heavily on my latest Norwegian popular science book (Thrane, 2024b).
2 Ritchie (2020) presents the story in its full length, and he also offers a treasure trove of other examples. See also https://en.wikipedia.org/wiki/Growth_in_a_Time_of_Debt
3 The story is simplified to tease out the gist. You find the full exposé here: https://www.newyorker.com/magazine/2023/10/09/they-studied-dishonesty-was-their-work-a-lie?fbclid=IwAR0jFqfcGxPwQzI8DvzPD56jCQy4XEJvbSL5Q1yGaYC3kPcism0myEo9r2I#sq_hife4q26ax.
4 See https://www.businessinsider.com/dan-ariely-duke-fraud-investigation-2024-2

5 Well, not quite. Salsburg (2017, pp. 125–126) came up with the original fraudulent data, which I took one step – or to be exact: one throw – further. I trust he also made the correct probability calculation.

6 See Ritchie (2020) for more on this.

7 Some scientific journals now demand that authors provide the original data when they submit a research paper. This is progress, obviously, but it is still not a bullet-proof strategy against data fabrication.

8 This topic is too large to be covered in detail, but here is the gist of it. After research has gone through peer review in a well-respected scientific journal, we can often be confident the statistical analyses used are the most suitable ones for the purposes at hand. Nonetheless, much, if not most, research appears in not-so-well-respected scientific journals, and the quality-testing procedures in even well-respected journals sometimes fail. Therefore, we cannot always trust the results of (statistical) research to be correct.

9 See Anscombe (1973). Notice that the averages and the standard deviations for the x-variables and y-variables yielding the four graphs also are similar. Mighty impressive!

10 Perhaps the most typical is that researchers report both absolute and relative risks, whereas journalists more often choose the relative ones to get a juicier story? Well, it is a hypothesis, at least.

11 This is more than simplification, as mentioned in Chapter 4. The regression coefficient either falls between 0.72 and 0.89 in the population or it does not. The correct interpretation of the 95 percent CI is less translucent: if we were to repeat the study many times over (taking repeated samples from the same population in the exact same manner) and calculate the CI for the regression coefficient each time, we expect 95 percent of the CIs to contain the true coefficient in the population. Breath out!

12 The CI is wider in areas where there are fewer units, in this example for tables with many diners. In general, there is more uncertainty when an analysis is based on few units, all else being equal. For this reason, the standard error increases and so does the 95 percent CI.

13 Cohen's w applies to a cross-tabulation of any size (e.g., 3×3, 4×4, etc.), and not just the 2×2 case. We might think of Cohen's w along the lines of a "correlation coefficient" for a cross-tabulation.

14 A random selection mechanism does not automatically create an unbiased sample. But it tends to do so in the long run. Conversely, samples not generated by a random selection procedure are almost always biased in some way.

15 Gladwell (2011) launched the analysis yielding this idea. De Mesquita and Fowler (2021), among several others, have severely criticized it later.

16 "Bullshit" is an academic word introduced by the philosopher Harry G. Frankfurt in a book in 2005, following up on an essay from 1986. Bergstrom and West (2020) have more on bullshit in a statistical (data) context.

17 There are alternatives to the RCT (and, more generally, to experimental designs) as a means of identifying a causal relationship. See Best and Wolf (2015), Cunningham (2021), Huntington-Klein (2022), and Rosenbaum (2017).

18 We have only analyzed cross-sectional data in this book. These are data referring to one point in time. Longitudinal data, in contrast, imply data collection at several points in time. When the same units (e.g., people, firms, countries) are examined for the same variables at several points in time, we have the so-called panel data. Analyzing panel data is beyond the scope of this book, but the statistical techniques involved generally do not differ much from the ones we have covered in this book.

19 Harford (2020) offers a similar list of questions.

20 The topics of how to handle missing data and outliers could also be added to this list. See, respectively, Aggerwal (2017) and Allison (2002). I also discuss outliers a bit more in Chapter 8.

FURTHER READING

I recommend Bergstrom and West (2020), Ritchie (2020), Kline (2020), and Harford (2020) as follow-ups to this chapter.

8

DOING YOUR OWN STATISTICAL RESEARCH PROJECT

INTRODUCTION

At some point in your life, you might have to make the leap from reading about statistical analysis to doing *your own* statistical analysis project. Well, we have now reached that point. This chapter kicks off with a walkthrough of the various phases in a typical statistical research project, to set the scene for the subsequent section of doing a regression research project. Next up, we are going to look at the so-called regression assumptions using our freshly completed project as a backdrop. To trust the results of a regression analysis, it must

DOI: 10.4324/9781032640808-8

meet certain assumptions of which several can be tested by using a statistics program. After this testing, the time has come to wrap up with some parting words.

THE PHASES OF A STATISTICAL RESEARCH PROJECT

Statistical research projects in the social and behavioral sciences often have lots in common. In fact, so much is common that it makes sense to think of a process that could be depicted in a schematic figure, like in Figure 8.1.1 If you are a bachelor's or master's student, the general statistical research project in the figure might align with your master's thesis project or bachelor's thesis project.

The first phase, which arguably is much more laborious and time-consuming than typically portrayed in most books on research methods, initially concerns crafting your study's research question. This question needs not to be singular. In fact, the research question is most often a short statement or summary of the *questions* you will address in your study. And based on what we have been through in this book so far, we are talking about the associational research questions introduced in Chapter 3.[2] (Some prefer the term research purpose rather than research question; I do not.)

Lots can be said about crafting a "good" research question. For starters, it is important to emphasize that a good research question does not just fall out of thin air. On the contrary, it often starts with some vague idea of statistical associations that somehow gradually transforms into a final research question, spurred by the reading of what other researchers have published on the topic of interest.[3] It might also happen that the reading-up on research will make your initial research question become superfluous. Sorry, but this occurs a lot! And then it is back to square one, where you must come up with a new and hopefully not-yet-answered research question. The gist of it all is that your final research question – often, but not necessarily, accompanied by a set of formal hypotheses – is the result of a mental but energy-demanding tug-of-war between your own thoughts and what prior research has documented.

But let's suppose that you, likely with the guidance of your supervisor, have managed to come up with a research question that is both doable and has some measure of originality. It thus warrants a master's or bachelor's thesis project. Now, the time has come to do some data collection.

In principle, you have two main options when it comes to data collection. You can choose to gather the data yourself, or you can use data already available in the sense that someone else has gathered the data for you. (One of these approaches is less laborious, guess which?) Neither I nor anyone else have a clear-cut answer to what is preferable in general. The reason is simple: there is no one-size-fits-all answer. Still, the pertinent question is whether your research question absolutely requires tailor-made and/or unique data. If the answer is yes, which it sometimes is, you should probably collect your own data. If the answer is no, then using available data pretty much speaks for itself.

If you go for gathering your own data, you often have two main options available: (1) collecting the data through a questionnaire or by using an experimental design or (2) collecting the data by some sort of "detective work" on for example the web.[4] Some years back, the latter was often a manual process. But with the emergence

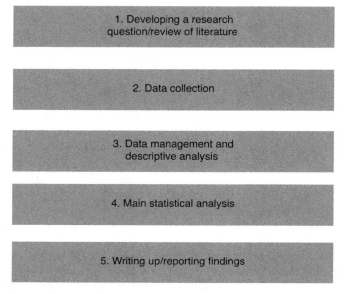

Figure 8.1 A statistical research project as a process or series of phases

of so-called web scraping procedures, this process is by now often entirely automated.[5]

If you decide to use available data for your statistical research project, you are essentially looking at an (almost) endless array of data sets. Many countries have national statistical agencies that store and distribute past level-of-living studies and the like for research purposes. In addition, there is an abundance of repositories around the world making (survey) data available for these purposes.[6] My gut feeling tells me that you in most cases will find something to your liking.

Whatever the source of your collected data, they will always require some cleaning and preparation. We have now reached the phase of data management and descriptive analysis, aka the getting-to-know-your-data stage. I'm not going to say much about data management and descriptive analysis as of right now, however.[7] But I most definitely have more to say on both topics when we later in this chapter look at a new and exemplary case study.

The fourth phase – the main statistical analysis – corresponds roughly to what we did in Chapters 3–6. I'll expand on this also in conjunction with the upcoming exemplary case study. The fifth and final phase – writing up and reporting – is something we have touched on throughout the whole book. But, as you might expect, I still have some more insights to offer later in the chapter.

The next section adds more meat to the bare-bones presentation of the research process outlined above. That is, we'll develop a research question in a "dialogue" with extant research, collect our data, do the descriptive analyses, do the main analyses, and write up our findings and conclusions.

AN EXEMPLARY REGRESSION STUDY ON THE DETERMINANTS OF TRANSFER FEES IN FOOTBALL

In football (soccer), success and monetary investment go hand in hand. Clubs with larger budgets generally outperform those with smaller ones, and the best players are invariably involved in the highest-priced transfers. These phenomena are also interconnected. Wealthier clubs have more money to spend on acquiring top-tier players, and by offering these players substantial salaries to secure their loyalty, these affluent clubs often become the highest performing ones. Our research question lies in identifying some of the key factors contributing to the variation in transfer fee amounts. For obvious reasons by now, perhaps, our focus is on the Norwegian football transfer market. With the research process sketched up in the last section as a backdrop, let's proceed:

The initial, vague research question. Based on our rudimentary knowledge of labor markets in football, we have come up with three initial-gut associations that might make it all the way to a final research question. (1) Contract length should affect transfer fees. After the so-called Bosman ruling, a player can change club for free if he (or she) is no longer under contract. It follows that players with much time left in their contracts should sell for more on average than players with less time left in their contracts. (2) Top-tier match experience should affect transfer fees. On average, more experienced players should sell for more than less experienced players. But perhaps only up to certain age point? (3) Is there an import-export difference? Since there are much larger monetary investments in, say, the Big-Five leagues (Premier League in England, La Liga in Spain, Serie A in Italy, Bundesliga in Germany, and Ligue 1 in France) than in the Norwegian top-tier league, we should expect that export transfer fees are higher than import transfer fees. How big – or small – is this transfer fee difference on average?

Developing a research question / review of literature. After a quick search on Google scholar (search words: transfer fees football), I found three recent studies providing the necessary background for assessing our vague research question above:[8]

McHale, I. G., and Holmes, B. (2023). Estimating transfer fees of professional footballers using advanced performance metrics and machine learning. *European Journal of Operational Research*, 306, 389–399.

Poli, R., Besson, R., and Ravenel, L. (2022). Econometric approach to assessing the transfer fees and values of professional football players. *Economies*, 10, 1–14.

Yang, Y, Koenigstorfer, J., and Pawlowski, T. (2022). Predicting transfer fees in professional European football before and during COVID-19 using machine learning. *European Sport Management Quarterly*, 24, 603–623.

Regarding contract length's effect on transfer fees, these studies show that we are onto something. The Poli–study also stresses that remaining contract length is a key x-variable in terms of explaining variation in transfer fee amounts. Even more so, the study suggests that *not* taking contract length into account when "predicting" transfer fees is a major flaw in several prior studies on the subject.

The three studies also show that match experience at the top-tier level is relevant for explaining variation in transfer fee amounts. Yet whether this relationship is mostly linear or non-linear (an inverted U) appears to be an open question. Lastly, the import-export difference is also unresolved: no prior study has explicitly examined this. That said, both the Poli–study and the Yang-study find that buyer and seller clubs' financial strength matters for transfer fees, much as expected. Furthermore, the three studies point toward relevant control variables when associating any x-variable with transfer fees. These control variables typically fall into one of three groups: (1) player characteristics, (2) performance variables, and (3) situational factors (e.g., buyer club characteristics, seller club characteristics, time effects). To summarize, our initially vague research question seems to fil a gap in extant research. As such, it warrants the designation of a final research question as well.[9] Coming up is data collection.

Data collection. The data to be analyzed were extracted manually from the German website called https://www.transfermarkt.com/.[10] The data cover all import and export transfers from the Norwegian top-tier league in the period from 2015 to 2023 (N = 311). In this sense, the data are a population rather than a sample. The number of transfers for each year ranges from 17 (2015) to 82 (2023).

Data management and descriptive data analysis. The data management process mainly boiled down to checking for any extreme outliers or other "strange" numbers in the spreadsheet, the labeling of variables, and the recoding of certain variables. I have provided an endnote with more details.[11] As for the descriptive data analysis, we typically begin with the characteristics of the dependent variable or y-variable, namely the transfer fee amount variable in our exemplary data. Table 8.1 presents the most relevant descriptive results.

While the average transfer fee is almost 12 million NOK according to Table 8.1, the median transfer fee is just south of 6 million NOK. This huge difference suggests a right-skewed distribution, which the histogram in Figure 8.2 confirms. The standard deviation is roughly 16 million NOK.[12]

Figure 8.2 tells us that very few players are involved in transfers exceeding 30 million NOK. The exact number is 26 players. Only three transfers – Hugo Vetlesen (90 millions), Erling Braut Haaland (93 millions), and David Datro Fofana (128 millions) – exceeded 90 million NOK fees. These "expensive players" pull the mean transfer fee upward and away from the median transfer fee. In contrast, 258 players, or 83 percent of them, were involved in transfers in which the fee was lower than 20 million NOK.

The information in Table 8.1 and Figure 8.2 suggests that we should use the logarithm (Ln) of transfer fee as the y-variable in our study; cf. special topic 1 in Chapter 5. Figure 8.3 shows the distribution for this Ln transfer fee variable by way of another histogram. We

Table 8.1 Descriptive statistics for transfer fee variable. N = 311

	Mean	Median	SD	Min	Max
Transfer fee (NOK mill.)	11.797	5.924	16.061	0.108	128.066

Note. All transfer fees are adjusted to 2023 NOK by the Consumer Price Index (CPI). NOK 100 has traditionally been the equivalent of roughly €10 or $11.

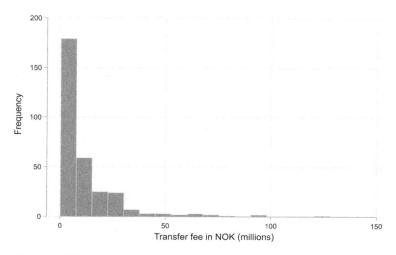

Figure 8.2 Histogram of transfer fees

notice that the logarithmic fee variable has a much more symmetric distribution than its natural equivalent.

Now, let's turn to descriptive statistics for our three key *x*-variables. Table 8.2 presents the relevant output for remaining contract length and total number of matches played on a top-tier level in career.

Table 8.2 shows that the average remaining contract length is about 20 months (mean), whereas the average player has 17 months left of his contract (median), with a range from 1.03 to 64.06 months.

In the same manner, the average top-tier match experience is 73 matches, with a range from 0 to 279 matches. The average player, in contrast, has played 61 top-tier matches (median). Descriptive statistics for our third *x*-variable is displayed in Table 8.3.

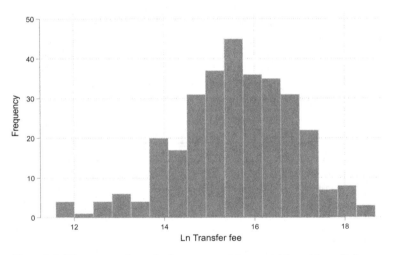

Figure 8.3 Histogram of transfer fees expressed in natural logarithms (Ln)

Table 8.2 Descriptive statistics for remaining contract length and top-tier matches played. N = 311

	Mean	Median	SD	Min	Max
Contract length (months)	19.67	17.16	11.69	1.03	64.06
Matches played	72.74	61.00	54.64	0	279

Perhaps not surprisingly, the mode in Table 8.3 is export transfers. More than half of the transfers, or 52 percent of them to be exact, were export transfers. We are now ready for the main statistical analysis phase.

Main statistical analysis: introduction. We are closing in on the finals, as in the contents of Chapters 3–6. In the first part of this phase, we usually associate our y-variable to our key x-variables one by one. Tables 8.4–8.6 take us through the particulars. With any luck this sets the stage and points to the conclusion of our main story.

Table 8.4 associates the logarithm of the transfer fee variable to the remaining contract length variable. Now, the thing to remember from Chapter 5 is that the regression coefficient refers to a difference in *percent*. We note that a player who has, say, 20 months left of his contract has a 3.5 percent higher transfer fee than a player who has 19 months left of his contract. In other words, the transfer fee *decreases* by an average of 3.5 percent for each new month a player closes in on contract termination. This association is statistically significant, with a very low p-value. Figure 8.4 shows the results in Table 8.4 graphically.

In a similar fashion, Table 8.5 presents how transfer fee (Ln) is associated with number of top-tier matches played, and Figure 8.5 shows these results visually.

Table 8.3 Frequency table for type of transfer variable. N = 311

Type of transfer	Frequency	Frequency in percent	Cumulative percent
Import transfer	63	21	21
Export transfer	163	52	73
Internal transfer	85	27	100

Table 8.4 Transfer fee (Ln) by remaining contract length. Linear regression

Independent variables	
Remaining contract length (months)	0.035 (0.006)★★★
Constant	14.899
R^2	0.102
N	311

Note. Standard errors are in parentheses.

★ $p < 0.05$; ★★ $p < 0.01$; ★★★ $p < 0.001$ (two-tailed tests).

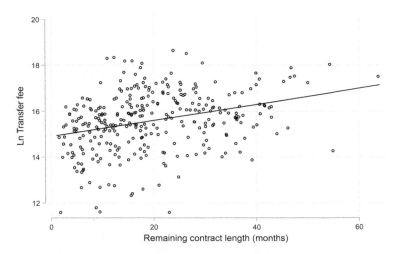

Figure 8.4 Transfer fee (Ln) by remaining contract length. Graph based on the results of Table 8.4

Table 8.5 Transfer fee (Ln) by top-tier matches played. Linear regression

Independent variables	
Matches played	0.012 (0.004)★★
Matches played-squared (× 1000)	−0.046 (0.018)★★
Constant	15.128
R^2	0.034
N	311

Note. Standard errors are in parentheses.

★ $p < 0.05$; ★★ $p < 0.01$; ★★★ $p < 0.001$ (two-tailed tests).

The combined results of Table 8.5 and Figure 8.5 suggest a tendency in the direction of an inverted U-pattern between top-tier match experience and transfer fees. The top-inflection point is at about 100 matches. Both regression coefficients are statistically significant at conventional levels.

Lastly, Table 8.6 associates the type of transfer to the logarithm of transfer fee. Due to the size of the coefficients, these must be transformed to become correct percent differences (cf. Chapter 5). Export transfers are thus 107 percent higher-priced than import

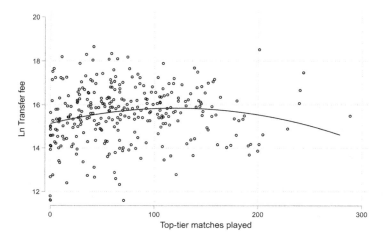

Figure 8.5 Transfer fee (Ln) by top-tier matches played. Graph based on the results of Table 8.5

Table 8.6 Transfer fee (Ln) by type of transfer. Linear regression

Independent variables	
Type of transfer[a]	
Export transfer (= 1)	0.728 (0.170)★★★
Internal transfer (= 1)	−0.602 (0.190)★★★
Constant	15.369
R^2	0.203
N	311

Note. Standard errors are in parentheses.

[a] Reference = Import transfer.

★ $p < 0.05$; ★★ $p < 0.01$; ★★★ $p < 0.001$ (two-tailed tests).

transfers (($100 \times (2.71828^{0.728}-1)) \approx 107$ percent). Following the same procedure, internal transfers are 45 percent lower-priced than import transfers (($100 \times (2.71828^{-0.602}- 1)) = -45.23$). Both regression coefficients are statistically significant, with very low p-values. This information is in no need of a figure.

Main statistical analysis: the finals. Chapter 5 taught us at least one fundamental thing: to find the *unique* effect of x_1 on y, we should control for x_2, x_3, x_4, and so on. Table 8.7 is a first attempt at such control. The multiple regression results in Table 8.7 generally support the findings of Tables 8.4–8.6. Remaining contract length continues to positively affect transfer fees, top-tier match experience maintains an inverse U-relationship with transfer fees, and type of transfer (i.e., import, export, internal) still influences transfer fees. Combined, these three x-variables explain roughly 29 percent of the variation (variance) in transfer fees (Ln).[13]

The three studies in the literature review provided us with some pointers regarding necessary control variables when examining variation in transfer fees: player characteristics, performance variables, and situational factors (e.g., buyer club characteristics, seller club characteristics, time effects). The multiple regression model reported in Table 8.8 takes several of these control variables into account.

Table 8.8 displays several findings. Adjusted for a host of relevant control variables, our three key x-variables continue to have statistically significant effects on transfer fees. Remaining contract length affect transfer fees positively, top-tier match experience has an inverse U-relationship with transfer fees, and type of transfer influences transfer fees. Among the control variables, four results stand out as essential:[14] (1) age matters for transfer fees. Older players are sold or bought for less money than younger ones. For instance,

Table 8.7 Transfer fee (Ln) by key independent variables. Multiple linear regression

Independent variables	
Remaining contract length (months)	0.032 (0.005)★★★
Matches played	0.009 (0.003)★★
Matches played-squared (× 1000)	−0.033 (0.016)★
Type of transfer[a]	
Export transfer (= 1)	0.655 (0.163)★★★
Internal transfer (= 1)	−0.479 (0.182)★★
Constant	14.387
R^2	0.294
N	311

Note. Standard errors are in parentheses.

[a] Reference = Import transfer.

★ $p < 0.05$; ★★ $p < 0.01$; ★★★ $p < 0.001$ (two-tailed tests).

players in the 25-to-26-year category are sold or bought for 60 percent less than players in the under 21 years category (($100 \times (2.71828^{-0.906}-1)) = -59.58$). (2) Goal-scoring matters for transfer

Table 8.8 Transfer fee (Ln) by key independent variables and controls. Multiple linear regression

Independent variables	
Remaining contract length (months)	0.026 (0.005)★★★
Matches played	0.013 (0.003)★★★
Matches played-squared (× 1000)	−0.055 (0.016)★★
Type of transfer[a]	
Export transfer (= 1)	0.474 (0.161)★★★
Internal transfer (= 1)	−0.459 (0.181)★
Age group[b]	
21–22 years (= 1)	−0.281 (0.176)
23–24 years (= 1)	−0.417 (0.195)★
25–26 years (= 1)	−0.906 (0.225)★★★
27 years or more (= 1)	−1.097 (0.262)★★★
Player position[c]	
Midfielder (= 1)	−0.073 (0.143)
Attacker (= 1)	0.059 (0.169)
National team appearance (no = 0; yes = 1)	0.081 (0.147)
Number of goals	0.013 (0.004)★★
Number of assists	0.004 (0.008)
Number of Champions League matches	−0.002 (0.025)
Number of Europa League matches	0.026 (0.012)★
Year	0.085 (0.022)★★★
Top-three ranked buying club (no = 0; yes = 1)	0.630 (0.117)★★★
Top-three ranked seller club (no = 0; yes = 1)	0.223 (0.131)
Constant	−157.87
R^2	0.506
N	311

Note. Standard errors are in parentheses. The regression also controls for player nationality (four dummies).

[a] Reference = Import transfer.

[b] Reference = Under 21 years.

[c] Reference = Keeper/defender.

★ $p < 0.05$; ★★ $p < 0.01$; ★★★ $p < 0.001$ (two-tailed tests).

fees. One more goal scored suggests a 1.3 percent higher transfer fee. (3) Year of transfer matters for transfer fees. For each year closer to the present, fees get 8.5 percent higher. (4) Club characteristics matter for transfer fees. If a top-three ranked club is involved as a buyer, the fee is 88 percent higher than if such a club is not involved at all $((100 \times (2.71828^{0.630}-1)) = 87.76)$. In total, the x-variables explain about 50 percent of the variation in transfer fees ($R^2 = 0.506$).

Much more could probably be said about the multiple regression results in Table 8.8. For starters, we have the 95 percent confidence intervals, the effect sizes, the possible interaction effects, and the possible non-linear effects. But since we already have covered these in detail in earlier chapters, I see no reason to push the repeat button here.

Writing up/reporting findings. In a sense, this is what we indirectly have been doing all along in this chapter. But now I'm thinking about how statistical research typically is written up in papers to be published in scientific journals (hopefully). One popular way of structuring the research of the type presented in this chapter is the so-called IMRaD setup: Introduction, Methods, Results, and Discussion. That said, many social science papers also include a separate Theory/Literature review section between the Introduction section and the Methods section. Perhaps for obvious reasons, this way of organizing the reporting of research has lots in common with the research process depicted in Figure 8.1. But the overlap is not quite one to one, as we now shall see.

When applying the IMRaD setup to our football transfer fee project, it is obvious that our research question belongs in the Introduction section. With no separate Theory/Literature review section, it is equally obvious that our (very short) literature review also belongs in the introduction. Generally, the Introduction section is where we answer the question of why we have done our research project in the first place: what makes our study interesting from a scientific and/or policy point of view? Many introductions finish off with a set of hypotheses or, more generally, with some expectations of what results to find. Some also reveal these main findings at the tail end of the Introduction section. Different scientific journals – as well as different scientific fields – have different ways of structuring their research papers. A piece of advice for free and up front: make sure knowing how your chosen journal prefers things *before* submitting your research paper.

The Method section contains all things having to with the data collection and the choices made in the data analysis phase. Obviously, this section is the place we have been "working within" most of the time in this book. For example, tables of descriptive statistics, such as Tables 8.1–8.3, belong here. The Results section not only has a telling name. It is also the section where the main analyses' results are explicated to readers, akin to how I presented the results of Tables 8.7 and 8.8 a few paragraphs back.

The Discussion section follows lastly. This is typically the place for the interpretation and discussion of the study's main results with theory and/or prior research as the backdrop. But it is also the place for any policy-relevant implications the study might have.[15] And it is, perhaps unsurprisingly by now, where any wrongful (policy) interpretations typically pop up; cf. Chapter 7.

Much can go wrong in a regression-based research project along the lines of the football transfer fee study we just conducted. Fortunately, many such wrongdoings can be avoided if we make sure our "final" regression model lives up to some formal criteria. In regression speak, this is a matter of our regression model not violating the regression assumptions. Hang on now, we are closing in on the finish line!

THE REGRESSION ASSUMPTIONS

To get a grip of the regression assumptions, it is probably wise to focus the exposition on one specific x-variable. I have chosen the remaining contract length variable as x_1 for this purpose. The question to be answered is thus: how can we be certain that contract length's regression coefficient in Table 8.8, b_1 or 0.026, is an *unbiased* effect on transfer fees?[16] There are three main types of regression assumptions to consider: (A) the non-testable assumptions for b_1's unbiasedness, (B) the testable assumptions for b_1's unbiasedness, and (C) the assumptions for making a correct assessment of b_1's statistical significance. Of these, in my opinion at least, the two formers are much more scientifically important than the latter.

A. *The non-testable assumptions for b_1's unbiasedness.* Non-testable, it should be pointed out, implies non-testable within our statistics program. The first non-testable assumption reads:

- The (multiple) regression model includes all relevant x-variables.

This assumption says that if we are to trust that b_1 is unbiased, the regression model it is a part of should contain all relevant x-variables. In our context, this means that the regression coefficient of 0.026 in Table 8.8 is unbiased *only* if the multiple regression model includes all relevant x-variables affecting transfer fees.[17] But as explained in Chapters 5 and 6, we can never be 100 percent sure that this is, in fact, the case. We cannot know what would happen to the contract length coefficient if some unknown x-variable was added to the regression in Table 8.8; hence the untestable character of this nevertheless crucial assumption.[18] The second non-testable assumption reads:

- The (multiple) regression model does not include any irrelevant x-variables.

This assumption is less critical. In practice, it also plays little role since most regression models (in the social and behavioral sciences, at least) typically include some non-relevant x-variables. This becomes obvious if you think about it for a second: we typically use regression to examine whether some specific x-variable is relevant for explaining variation in y or not. The player position and national team appearance variables in Table 8.8 would appear to be such variables. But they became "irrelevant" (as in not significant) only *after* we had run our regression. Before that moment, the literature review clearly stated that these variables should be among the *relevant* control variables.

B. *The testable assumptions for b_1's unbiasedness.* We have now reached the doings of our statistics program. There are four key assumptions for b_1's unbiasedness in *linear* regression:

- Linearity
- No multicollinearity
- No influential outliers
- Additivity (i.e., no interaction effects)

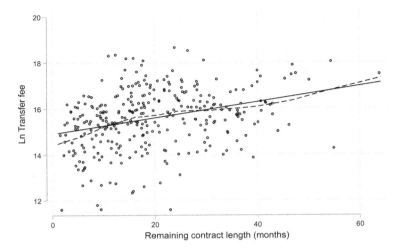

Figure 8.6 Transfer fee (Ln) by remaining contract length. Graph based on the results of Table 8.4. The dashed line is the data-driven trend line; the solid line is the linear regression line

The first testable assumption, *linearity*, is obvious given the name "linear regression." There should be an approximate linear association between x_1 and y in the data. We have already seen in Figure 8.4 that this was the case for the contract length variable. Figure 8.6 provides a data-driven trend line (cf. Chapter 3) alongside the linear regression line. The conclusion seems evident. The relationship between contract length and transfer fees is linear for all intents and purposes.[19] But what if this x_1-y relationship is not linear? That is, what if the linearity assumption is violated? Well, then we should instead try using some kind on non-linear regression approach, as we did in Chapter 5. Or, more recently, as we did for the total number of top-tier matches variable; cf. Table 8.5 and Figure 8.5.

Despite its gibberish name, the *no multicollinearity* assumption is easy to grasp when we have seen some multiple regression models in action. Multicollinearity refers to a situation in which there are too strong "correlations" among our x-variables. (Quotes are used to stress that correlation normally is a term to describe an association between two quantitative variables. But now we are describing associations between x-variables on all levels of measurement.) The intuition is straightforward. Let's say you want to estimate a multiple regression model where yearly wage is y, and where age and years of work experience are, respectively, x_1 and x_2. The problem with this model, at least for most of the employees in your data, is that when a person gets one more year of work experience, he or she also becomes one year older. This is a classic example of a "perfect" correlation between x_1 (age) and x_2 (work experience). The result? The regression model won't be able to separate the effects of age and work experience on wage. And that is why we in the presence of multicollinearity cannot claim that the b_1 and b_2 our statistic program still churns out reflect the unique or partial effect of x_1 and x_2 on y. On the flip side: when "correlations" between x-variables are tolerable (for lack of a better word), this ability of separating the effects of x_1 and x_2 on y is regression's strongest forte.

Thankfully, the situation of almost perfect multicollinearity is uncommon. The more typical situation is that "correlations" become so high that they get worrisome. The so-called VIF (Variation Inflation Factor) has become the standard way of assessing "degree" of multicollinearity. A much-cited rule-of-thumb says that the mean VIF-score — that is, the VIF-score among all the x-variables in the regression model — should not exceed 10. But since I have yet to see any empirical footing for this VIF-score threshold, I follow the advice of some very notable researchers and practice a much lower rule-of-thumb value: mean VIF-scores above 4 or 5 are typically worrisome.[20]

One frequent special case is worth mentioning for the assessment of VIF-scores. When regression models include squared variables to examine non-linear effects (e.g., matches played and matches played-squared in Table 8.8), the VIF-score by necessity gets an upward boost. This is a mathematical consequence of the high correlation between the original variable and its squared term.[21] In situations like these, it is usually more prudent to test for the mean VIF-score without the squared variable. The mean VIF-score for the regression model in Table 8.8 is 1.90 without the variable matches played-squared.[22] This VIF-score is unproblematic no matter how you choose to look at it. The multicollinearity assumption is not violated.

What to do, then, when the multicollinearity assumption gets violated? There is no magic bullet. Do nothing is sound advice if the "questionable" variables have (theoretically) reasonable coefficients that are statistically significant at conventional levels. Whenever possible, it can also be worthwhile to add more units to the analysis. A third option is to remove the x-variable or x-variables that is/are the root of the problem. But this option might get you into conflict with the first and untestable regression assumption, namely that the multiple regression model should include *all* relevant x-variables.[23]

The assumption of *no influential outliers* implies that the magnitude of the regression coefficient, b_1, is not a consequence of any extreme outliers – like in Figure 7.1. Stated differently, if we remove the units located very far away from the "typical" units in the data, the size of the regression coefficient should not change by much. A graphical inspection of the data, like in Figure 8.6, often get us a long way in terms of spotting potential influential outliers. In contrast, when analyzing large data sets, visual inspection is less than optimal. In these circumstances, the only viable option for identifying possibly influential outliers is to let your statistics program do the work for you.[24]

Before trying the perhaps obvious solution of removing outliers, however, you should always ask why this or that data point is in this or that location. Is it a data entry error? If yes, then deleting is both ok and sensible. If not, well, deleting data points requires some sort of theoretical justification. At its core, how to handle influential outliers is not a statistical problem. It is much more of a data or data representativeness problem.

One apparent solution to possibly disturbing outliers is to estimate a regression model that keeps the influence of outliers as little as possible. This, in essence, is what the so-called *robust* regression does. If I instruct my statistics program to estimate a robust counterpart of the regression in Table 8.8, I obtain a coefficient of 0.024 for the contract length variable. Practically speaking, this is the same result as the one reported in Table 8.8. Figure 8.6 and the results of the robust regression procedure suggest the conclusion that our regression model meets the assumption of no influential outliers.

The *additivity* assumption is something we already have encountered and solved in the book. Simply stated, additivity means that our regression model is meaningful and in sync with reality *without* any interaction terms being present in the model. If this is not the case (and we thus have a violation of additivity), we should extend our regression model by means of one or more interaction terms – just as we did in Chapter 5. End of story.

C. *The assumptions for making a correct assessment of b_1's statistical significance.* These assumptions, the arguably not-so-important ones, all concern the regression equation's error term, *e*, which briefly was mentioned in passing in the appendix to Chapter 3. Recall that the general bivariate regression model should be written as:

$$y = b_0 + b_1 x + e,$$

where *e* accounts for random variation and all other *x*-variables' effects on *y*. In short, this *e* should be:

-   Homoscedastic (i.e., have a constant variance)
-   Normally distributed (i.e., follow the Gauss distribution)
-   Uncorrelated (i.e., be independent of each other)

In practice, we test these assumptions by assessing the so-called *residual*, which we may think of as *e*'s sample counterpart. More technically, the residual is a variable that gets computed but stays in the background of the statistics program every time we run a regression analysis. Before turning to these assumptions, I again emphasize that any violations do not affect the unbiasedness of b_1. They just complicate the assessment of b_1's statistical significance.

Homoscedasticity – or no heteroscedasticity (another two gibberish names, sorry) – essentially means that the spread around the regression line should be constant for the various levels of the *x*-variable. When they are not, we have heteroscedasticity, which is a violation of the homoscedasticity assumption. Let's take a first look at this up against the regression model appearing in Table 8.4. Figure 8.7 shows us the results. In Figure 8.7, which is called a residual versus fitted plot (I'm not kidding), the regression line is transformed into a horizontal line crossing the *y*-axis at $y = 0.035$ (i.e., the regression coefficient). And as a first brush stroke, we see that the spread around the regression line does not deviate much from being "constant." Yet for the larger *x*-values appearing on the right-hand side of the figure, the spread seems to decrease somewhat.

Since we now have a feel of what homoscedasticity versus heteroscedasticity is all about, we can ask for a similar residual versus fitted plot based on our "final" regression model in Table 8.8. This plot is displayed in Figure 8.8. In contrast to Figure 8.7, Figure 8.8

does not have one *x*-variable, but many. As such, any random pattern suggests homoscedasticity, whereas any systematic pattern suggests heteroscedasticity. On balance, the pattern in Figure 8.8 seems more

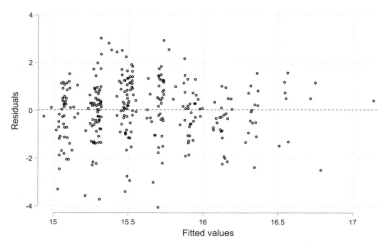

Figure 8.7 A residual versus fitted plot, based on the results of Table 8.4

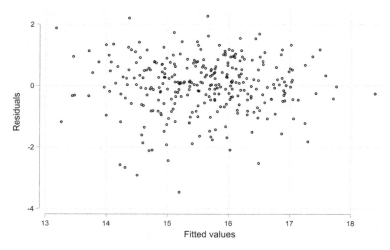

Figure 8.8 A residual versus fitted plot, based on the results of Table 8.8

or less random. We tentatively conclude that the regression model in Table 8.8 does not violate the homoscedasticity assumption.[25]

But for the argument's sake, suppose we face a homoscedasticity violation. What is the result of this violation? Recall from Chapter 4 that we found the t-value by dividing the regression coefficient by its standard error (b_1/SE). We also said that when this t-value was larger than 1.96 or smaller than -1.96, we rejected the null hypothesis and deemed our coefficient to be "statistically significant" in large samples. When heteroscedasticity enters the picture, the problem is that the usual way of computing the SE (by the statistics program, mind you) does *not* provide us with the correct SE. Suppose your regression coefficient is 10, and that its SE is 4. The t-value is thus 2.5 ($10/4 = 2.5$); we are talking about a statistically significant coefficient. Yet in the presence of heteroscedasticity, we know that this SE is incorrect. It could be larger, or it could be smaller, but the former is more usual in my experience. Say the correct SE is 6, and not 4. The correct t-value is thus 1.67 ($10/6 = 1.67$). That is, the correct t-value suggests that the regression coefficient in question is *not* statistically significant. The upshot? In the face of heteroscedasticity, we risk labeling a regression coefficient as statistically significant when it is not.[26]

What do we do in a situation of heteroscedasticity? It is time for remedies. Two solutions dominate in present-day statistical research. The first is more obvious: we compute a "new type" of SE that is correct even in the presence of heteroscedasticity. This was by no means a simple doing 20 years back, but today all comprehensive statistics programs calculate what is known in the lingo as a "robust" SE. And when doing this, we obtain the correct t-value in the usual manner. Problem solved, let's move on![27]

The second common solution involves transforming the y-variable, which in many cases reduces or eliminates any heteroscedasticity problem. So, when we in our case study some paragraphs back used the logarithm of transfer fees rather than the original transfer fee variable as our y-variable, we adopted a well-known procedure of mitigating heteroscedasticity.[28] (How cool is that?)

Normally distributed residuals imply, well, just that: if we were to graph the residuals in a histogram, they should follow the normal distribution we have seen on several occasions throughout this book. If we do this for our regression in Table 8.8, we get the histogram displayed in Figure 8.9.

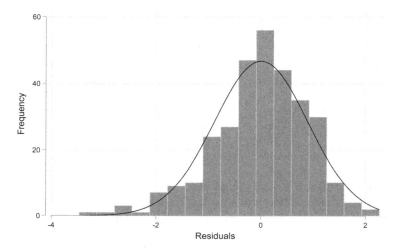

Figure 8.9 Histogram of the residuals resulting from the regression in Table 8.8, with normal distribution superimposed

Although the histogram in Figure 8.9 has some resemblance with a perfect normal distribution, it is *not* normally distributed in the strict sense. In other words, the normality assumption is violated.[29] What are the consequences of such a violation? And what are the remedies?

At the outset, the consequence of a normality assumption violation is that we no longer can trust our significance test to be correct – akin to how a homoscedasticity violation led to the same problem. In practice, however, this is a problem only for a small sample. For a large sample, we can invoke the Central Limit Theorem (CLT) explicated in the appendix to Chapter 3. So, when dealing with large samples, any violation of the normality assumption has no practical consequences to speak of. These considerations leave the normality assumption as a small-sample problem only. The remedies include trying out other statistical techniques than regression or transforming the *y*-variable in some way.[30]

The final assumption states that the residuals should be *uncorrelated* with each other. What does this mean? To answer this question in an intuitive way, it might be wise to take a step back for a moment. Consider our random sample of adult Norwegians scrutinized several times in this book, and how often or seldom these adults visited the doctor; cf. Chapter 5. Due to the random sampling procedure, we can be pretty sure that the number of times "Peter" visited the doctor did not affect (or was not affected by) how many times "George" visited the doctor, and so on. This, in essence, is what uncorrelated residuals imply: one unit's response to a y-variable is *independent* of another unit's response to the same y-variable. Now, say you have questionnaire data on all the pupils in a primary school, and that the y-variable is the assessment of the teaching environment as seen from the pupils' point of view. Will these pupils' answers be independent of each other? Probably not, since especially pupils going in the same class will share much of the same teaching environment. This is known as the "clustering" of units in the lingo: the response to a y-variable might be a function of the larger cluster to which a unit belongs.[31]

Let's recircle back to our data in this chapter. Could it happen that some cluster-effects are lurking in the background? For instance, is it possible that the transfer fees are affected by, say, the different (?) "import-export policies" of the Norwegian clubs being involved in the transfers? Well, this might be possible – at least to serve as an illustration of the more general point in question. If so, what are the consequences of the uncorrelated residuals violation? And what are the remedies? As in the case of heteroscedasticity and non-normal residuals, we cannot trust the significance test to be correct. Yes, the infamous and incorrect SE strikes back! The remedy – hold on tight – is to compute a so-called "cluster-robust" SE, which all sophisticated statistics programs have canned solutions for. But this straightforward solution only helps if have some way of identifying the "clusters" in our data. In our exemplary case data, we have the possibility to compute SEs taking the various Norwegian clubs into account. What happens if I re-estimate the regression model in Table 8.8 using cluster-robust SEs? Well, the SEs of the import-export dummies decrease in size, causing the t-values to increase. So, our p-values got lower *in this case*, which is a lot more fulfilling than the reverse.

Table 8.9 summarizes the main regression assumptions explicated above.

Table 8.9 A summary of the assumptions for linear regression analysis

---

(A) The non-testable assumptions for b_1's unbiasedness:

The (multiple) regression model includes all relevant x-variables

The (multiple) regression model does not include any irrelevant x-variables

(B) The testable assumptions for b_1's unbiasedness:

Linearity

No multicollinearity

No influential outliers

Additivity (i.e., no interaction effects)

(C) The assumptions for making a correct assessment of b_1's statistical significance:

Residuals should be homoscedastic (i.e., have a constant variance)

Residuals should be normally distributed (i.e., follow the Gauss distribution)

Residuals should be uncorrelated (i.e., be independent of each other)

FINAL WORDS

In the opening of this book, I said three things (ok, I said a lot more, but let's not split hairs):

1 I hope to show that doing statistical analysis can be interesting and worthwhile. Sometimes it is also exciting in the sense that learning something new can border on fun or at least be stimulating.

2 Practical statistical analysis is *not* about memorizing formulas, doing arithmetic calculations, and solving algebraic equations.

3 Practical statistical analysis is *not* difficult in the technical sense.

Have I delivered on my promise? That is up to you to decide and not me. But I can promise you that I have tried my very best to do so! In any event, good luck on reading more about statistical analysis and perhaps also doing it sometime in the future.

KEY LEARNING POINTS

The key learning points in this chapter were:

- The phases or steps of a statistical research project might be sub-divided into (1) developing a research question/review of literature, (2) data collection, (3) data management and descriptive analysis, (4) main statistical analysis, and (5) writing up/reporting of results.
- The above five phases or steps can be thought of as the (statistical) research process.
- Using an exemplary regression study on the determinants of transfer fees in football, this chapter has put some meat on the bones of the stylistic research process mentioned above.
- To be able to trust the results of a regression analysis, it must meet – as in not violate – a set of so-called regression assumptions.
- This chapter has also explicated these regression assumptions in detail, using an exemplary regression study on the determinants of transfer fees as a backdrop.

NOTES

1 There are numerous versions of this general setup of the (statistical) research process. This is my personal and stripped-down account. For a much more detailed version, see for example Clark et al. (2021).

2 There are other types of associational research questions than those covered in this book, just as there are other types of statistical techniques and other types of studies. But let's stay on the main path, shall we?

3 I would like to emphasize that the word "transforms" is a pitch-perfect description here.

4 I stress that these are the two typical *main* options.

5 See for example: https://medium.com/@spaw.co/best-websites-to-practice-web-scraping-9df5d4df4d1

6 See for example:
https://guides.lib.calpoly.edu/c.php?g=261997&p=1749797
https://dextutor.com/top-10-dataset-repositories/#google_vignette
https://libguides.mit.edu/socscidata/general

7 Data management is a large and necessary topic to master, but spending time describing it without doing it is a waste of time in my experience. So, more on this later in the chapter.

8 The McHale-study can be found here: https://www.sciencedirect.com/science/article/pii/S0377221722005082

The Poli-study can be found here:
https://www.mdpi.com/2227-7099/10/1/4

The Yang-study can be found here:
https://www.tandfonline.com/doi/full/10.1080/16184742.2022.2153898

You find a more general background study for player valuation in football here:
https://onlinelibrary.wiley.com/doi/epdf/10.1111/joes.12552?src=getftr

9 I'm not saying this was pure luck on my behalf. On the contrary, I did some preliminary "research" before coming up with this example.

10 Håkon Isak Amundsen and Jesper Flugind Lien began the data collection in 2023, and Fredrik Havnås and Simon Jonsson finished it in 2024. I sincerely thank them all for the permission to use the data in this educational setting.

11 When punching data in, say, Excel, we normally use short abbreviations as variable names on the top of the columns (e.g., trans_fee). Within our statistics program, we then typically assign labels to these variable names (e.g., Transfer fee in NOK). To create the variable tf_mill with the label Transfer fee in NOK (millions), I divided the variable trans_fee by 1,000,000. Similarly, I made the logarithmic variable log_tf with the label Ln Transfer fee by instructing my statistics program to take the natural logarithm of the trans_fee variable. I also recoded the import-export variable, so that import transfers were coded 0 (the reference), export transfers were coded 1, and internal (Norwegian) transfers were coded 2.

12 The interquartile range (IQR), the coefficient of variation (CV), and everything that has to do with Chapter 2 might be relevant descriptive statistics, but they do not necessarily belong in the story being told here. That is the only reason why I have left them out of the tables.

13 Note that the values of R^2 in Tables 8.4–8.6 are, respectively, 0.102, 0.034, and 0.203. When added up, they total 0.339 or 33.9 percent. However, the combined R^2 value in Table 8.7 is only 0.294 or 29.4 percent. How come? The reason is to be found in the associations between the three x-variables. The higher association among the x-variables, the larger the gap will be between the sum of the R^2 values for the individual x-variables and the R^2 for the regression model containing all the x-variables. More on these "associations" follows later in the chapter.

14 All upcoming effects have ceteris paribus interpretations that I omit for the benefit of a smoother presentation; cf. Chapter 5.

15 This is also the place for mentioning any of the limitations your study might have.

16 In principle, of course, the similar question should be asked for b_2 and b_3 (and so on). In practice, well, time and page space are in short supply.

17 Strictly correct, a *relevant* control variable is correlated with x_1 (contract length) and has its own, individual effect on y (transfer fee). If such a relevant control variable is missing for the regression model, we get omitted variable bias (in this case for the contract length variable). Earlier in this chapter, I mentioned that the Poli-study deemed all transfer fee regressions not controlling for contract length as "flawed." They might instead have said "suffering from omitted variable bias" without any loss of meaning.

18 As an office exercise, I added more x-variables to the model in Table 8.8 to see whether the contract length coefficient changed in magnitude. It appeared not to. But I could not – and cannot ever – add x-variables not being a part of my data.

19 Strictly correct, we should compare the data-driven trend line with the regression line yielded by the multiple regression in Table 8.8. But I can assure you that this alternate line looks very similar to the one portrayed in Figure 8.6.

20 Berk (2004) prefers a threshold value of roughly 5; Allison (1999) is even more conservative, preferring a threshold value of roughly 2.5. I am not as conservative as Allison.

21 The same problem comes up for interaction (i.e., product term) variables; cf. Chapter 5. Still, a high correlation between x_1 and x_1 multiplied by x_2 is not a multicollinearity problem.

22 The mean VIF-score is 2.84 when the squared term is included in the model. This is still not a multicollinearity problem.

23 Another remedy in the face of multicollinearity is to perform something called Ridge regression. See the further reading section.

24 See Meuleman et al. (2015) and Aggerwal (2017) for more on statistical techniques to detect and treat outliers in conjunction with regression modeling.

25 Well, a statistical test of homoscedasticity versus heteroskedasticity shows that we have a minor homoscedasticity violation. But, as shown later in this section, this has no practical consequences to speak of.

26 Or the other way around: to label a regression coefficient as not statistically significant when it is in fact statistically significant.

27 In our case, the "normal" and the "heteroskedasticity-robust" SEs are very similar. I see no reason to use page space on displaying this.

28 The so-called weighted least squares regression is another remedy; see Meuleman et al. (2015).

29 A formal test of significance also supports this: $p < 0.0001$.

30 Meuleman et al. (2015) have more to offer on this also.

31 The problem of correlated residuals typically comes up in regressions of panel data, i.e., data in which, say, persons are asked the same survey questions at several points in time. In such situations, the answer to question y at one point in time will probably be correlated with the answer to the same question y at a later or earlier point in time.

FURTHER READING

I recommend Gelman and Vehtari (2024), Aggerwal (2017), Allison (1999), Berk (2004), Thrane (2020), Best and Wolf (2015), and Meuleman et al. (2015) as follow-ups to this chapter.

GLOSSARY (WITH DATA-DRIVEN EXAMPLES)

Given this book's uncompromising preoccupation with actual data analysis, and to avoid tedious repetition, I recapitulate its key concepts using a new data set. The data refer to a random sample of Norwegian university students answering a questionnaire on certain lifestyle and health-related issues. There are 470 students in the sample. The variables and their definitions appear in Table G.1.

Table G.1 The variables in the student data and their definitions and codings. N = 470

Variable name	Variable definitions and codings	Average (mean)
Sex	Student's biological sex: female = 0, male = 1	0.39
Age	Student's age in years	23.16
Height (cm)	Student's height measured in centimeters	173.75
Weight (kg)	Student's weight measured in kilograms	72.25
Cardio	Student's hours of cardio exercise per week	2.01
Snuffing	Student's snuffing: no snuffing = 0, daily snuffer = 1	0.37
Health	Student's physical health status: ok = 0, good = 1, very good = 2	–

Italicized words refer to concepts that have been explained earlier or that will be explained later.

Association (variable association)   Statistical analysis has much to do with (1) examining whether there is an association between two *variables* and, if so, (2) describing the characteristics of this association.

Table G.2 Snuffing by biological sex. Cross-tabulation. Percentages

	Biological sex		
Daily snuffer (wet snuff)	Female	Male	Total
No	69	53	63
Yes	31	47	37
Total	100 (286)	100 (184)	100 (470)

Note. Numbers in parentheses are number of students.

Table G.2 is a *cross-tabulation* between the variables biological sex and daily snuffing.

Since the percentage or fraction of daily snuffers is clearly larger among the male students (47) than it is among the female students (31), there is an association between the *variables* biological sex and daily snuffing. We describe this association by pointing out that male students have a 16 percentage points larger probability of being snuffers than female students (47−31 = 16). A non-association would suggest that male and female students were daily snuffers to the (roughly) same extent.

Average (mean)   The average or mean is the most important measure of a *variable*'s central tendency. Such central tendency equals typicalness. Two other measures of central tendency are the *median* and the *mode*. The average applies to variables on the quantitative *measurement level*, i.e., quantitative *variables*. The average for the *variable* age in the student data is 23.16 years. We find this average by adding up the individual students' age and then divide the sum we get by 470 (the number of students in the *data*). Similarly, the average for the *variable* weight is 72.25 kilograms. Finally, the average for the variable number of cardio exercise hours per week is 2.01 hours.

Averages in two or more subgroups   Comparing averages among subgroups in the *data* is a typical statistical exercise. Table G.3, Panel A, compares the average of weight for the two biological sexes. Similarly, Panel B in Table G.3 compares the average of number of cardio exercise hours for the two sexes.

On average, male students weigh about 14 kilograms more than female students (81.01−66.61 = 14.40). Also, male students

Table G.3 Weight by biological sex (Panel A) and cardio exercise hours by biological sex (Panel B). N = 470

	Average
Panel A: weight (kg)	
Female	66.61 kg
Male	81.01 kg
Panel B: cardio exercise hours per week	
Female	1.71 hours
Male	2.48 hours

do 0.77 more cardio exercise hours per week than female students on average (2.48−1.71 = 0.77). The results in Table G.3 are examples of *associations* between two *variables*. A non–association would suggest that male and female students both weighed the same or did the same number of cardio exercise hours per week on average.

Coefficient of variation (CV)   Akin to the *standard deviation* or SD, the coefficient of variation or CV measures the variation around the average of a variable. To get the CV for the variable weight in the student *data*, we divide the SD of weight (13.25) by its average (72.25) and then multiply by 100: 18.34. The CV is most relevant when comparing the variation of *variables* having unequal *averages* and when comparing subgroups varying with respect to the *average*, such as for example weight among male and female students.

Confidence interval (CI), 95 percent   The student data pertain to a small percentage or subset of all students attending a university. We call this percentage or fraction a *sample*. In contrast, we call *all* the students attending a university a *population*. Given that a *sample* is the result of *random sampling* from a *population*, we use a 95 percent CI to find out what the (known) *sample* result most likely is for the (unknown) *population*. The *average* age among the students in the *sample* is 23.16. Given this *average*, the 95 percent CI suggests we are 95 percent confident that the *average* age in the student population falls in the range from 22.75 to 23.56 years (to simplify grossly; cf. Chapter 4). Similarly, given the *sample average* weight of 72.25

kilograms, we are 95 percent confident that the *average* weight in the student *population* is between 71.05 and 73.45 kilograms. All *sample* features have similar CIs.

Correlation and correlation coefficient   Correlation is a specific form of *association* between two *variables*. A correlation is an association between two quantitative *variables*. Figure G1 shows the correlation between students' weight (*y*-axis) and height (*x*-axis) in a scatterplot. We note a positive correlation: on *average*, taller students weigh more than shorter students. (Most students are located either in the upper right or in the lower left quadrant of the figure.) The strength of the correlation is measured by the correlation coefficient, which is 0.60. The correlation coefficient has a theoretical range from −1.00 (a perfect negative correlation) to 1.00 (a perfect positive correlation). A correlation of −1.00 or 1.00 implies that all data points fall on a straight line. The tighter the data points are scattered around this line, the larger the correlation coefficient tend to be (to simplify a bit).

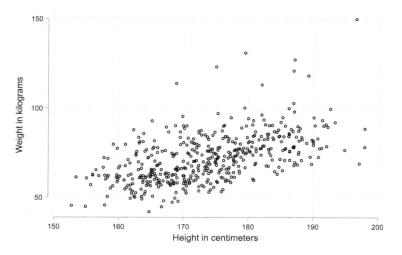

Figure G.1 Students' weight in kilograms by students' height in centimeters

Note. 70 inches (or 5 feet 10 inches) is roughly 178 centimeters.

Cross-tabulation   Table G.2 is a 2 × 2 cross-tabulation. A cross-tabulation shows the *association*, if any, between two variables having few possible values (categories) each. Cross-tables with more than, say, 16 or 20 cells (4 × 4 or 4 × 5) are generally hard to interpret.

Data (data set)   Data are the fuel of statistical analysis. Without data, there is no input for doing statistical exercises. Data or data sets are typically stored in spreadsheet-like matrixes organized in rows and columns. One row pertains to one *unit* in the data set (i.e., one student in our data). The columns in a data set refer to *variables*; one column is one variable. In survey questionnaire data, one column refers to the answer given to one question in the questionnaire.

Dependent variable (y-variable)   When associating two variables in statistics, we must specify the direction of the association: does variable A affect variable B, or does B affect A? The distinction between the dependent and the *independent variable* clarifies this. The dependent variable is being affected by the *independent variable*, in the sense that this is what we assume. In the correlation in Figure G1, the dependent weight variable on the *y*-axis is affected by the height variable on the *x*-axis. (That weight affects height makes no sense.) The dependent variable is often called the *y*-variable. In Table G.2, snuffing is the dependent variable; it is affected by biological sex. (The reverse makes no sense.)

Distribution   The distribution of a *variable* might be thought of as the visual description of the *variable's* frequency table. The two distributions for the *variables* cardio exercise hours per week and weight appear in, respectively, Figures G2 and G3.

   The distribution of the cardio exercise variable shows that exercising for zero hours per week is most typical, as per the tallest bar. This is the *mode*. Also, few students exercise for more than five hours per week. The cardio exercise *variable* has a right-skewed distribution; the *average* is larger than the *median* which, in turn, is larger than the *mode*. The weight variable has a more symmetric distribution around the *average* (mean) of 72.25 kilograms.

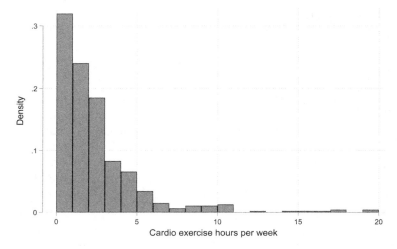

Figure G.2 Bar chart of students' cardio exercise hours per week

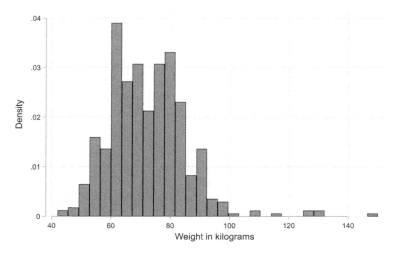

Figure G.3 Histogram of students' weight in kilograms

Effect size (effect-size measures) Effect-size measures are rule-of-thumb guidelines for assessing the strength of an *association* between two variables. In Table G.2, the effect size for the *association*

between daily snuffing and biological sex – Cohen's w – is about 0.16, making it a small effect. In Panel A in Table G.3, the effect size for the *association* between weight and biological sex – Cohen's d – is very large: 1.28. Finally, the *correlation coefficient* of 0.60 between weight and height in Figure G1 might be called a medium-sized effect.

Hypothesis   Hypothesis testing always concerns two hypotheses: the null hypothesis and the alternative hypothesis. The alternative hypothesis is what we believe in prior to the statistical analysis: some kind of systematic *association* between the two *variables* in question. The alternative hypothesis for the *association* between daily snuffing and biological sex in Table G.2 would (based on prior research) be that male students snuff more often than female students. The null hypothesis, in contrast, would state that there is no association between the two *variables* – or sex parity for the snuffing *variable*. The takeaway is that we in statistical analysis always test the null hypothesis. That is, we test what we in a sense do not expect by means of a *significance test*.

Independent variable (x-variable)   When associating two variables in statistics, we must specify the direction of the *association*: does variable A affect variable B, or does B affect A? The distinction between the independent and the *dependent variable* clarifies this choice. The *dependent variable* is being affected by the independent variable, in the sense that this is what we assume. In the correlation in Figure G1, the weight variable on the *y*-axis is affected by the independent height variable on the *x*-axis. (That weight affects height makes no sense.) The independent variable is often called the *x*-variable. In Table G.2, biological sex is the independent variable; it affects snuffing. (The reverse makes no sense.)

Mean (see average)

Measurement level   The measurement level of a *variable* dictates what kinds of statistical questions being relevant to ask.

Median   Second to the *average*, the median is the most used measure of central tendency for quantitative *variables*. We (as in our statistics program) do two operations to find the median. First, we sort the *units* for the variable in question in ascending order, such as the age or weight of the students. Then we find the *unit* in the middle of this age or weight *distribution*. These medians are, respectively, 22 years (the *average* is 23.15 years) and 71 kilograms (the *average* is 72.25 kilograms). When there are two units in the middle of a *distribution* – that is, for even *distributions* – the median is the *average* of these two middle units.

Medians in two or more subgroups   Comparing medians among subgroups in the *data* is a typical statistical exercise. We use a box and whisker plot in this regard, as shown in Figure G4. The information on the left-hand side pertains to the weight of the female students. The horizontal line in the middle of the box is the median: 65 kilograms. The box itself "contains" 50 percent of the female students in the data. The horizontal lines above and below the box are the whiskers. The weight range between upper and lower whisker includes almost all female students. We see one outlier (one hollow dot). This female student weighs a lot more than the rest of the female students. Similar information for the male students appears on the right-hand side of the figure. The median weight

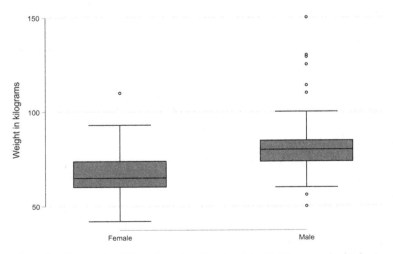

Figure G.4 Box and whisker plot of students' weight in kilograms, by biological sex

among the male students is 80 kilograms. There are several outliers among the male students.

Age (in years, months, weeks, …, milliseconds), height (in kilometers, meters, …, millimeters), and weight (in tons, kilograms, …, milligrams) are classic examples of quantitative *variables* – or *variables* on the quantitative measurement level. The quantitative measurement level sets the stage for most types of statistical analyses. The nominal measurement level is at the other end of the measurement level spectrum. Such *variables* have an either/or-logic to them, as in what day of the week it is (seven categories) or biological sex (two categories). Also, there is no ranking among the alternatives for a nominal *variable*. The special case is a nominal *variable* having only two categories, which is called a dummy *variable*. Save for dummy *variables*, the statistical analysis of nominal *variables* often boils down to counting how many *units* there are in each category of the *variable*. The third measurement level is the ordinal level. Ordinal *variables* share the property of nominal *variables* in terms of having few categories. Yet for ordinal *variables* there is a ranking among the alternatives. Table G.4 illustrates for the student data.

The students were asked to assess their overall physical health as ok, good, or very good. The table shows that most students (45 percent) define themselves in good health. This is also the *mode*. What makes this health *variable* ordinal is the ranking of the possible answer options: good is better than ok, and very good is better than good. In the main, ordinal variables make for more types of statistical analyses than nominal *variables*. Still, they are not quite as flexible as the quantitative *variables*.

Table G.4 Frequency table for physical health status. N = 470

Health status	Frequency	Frequency in percent	Cumulative percent
Ok	179	36	38
Good	223	47	86
Very good	68	14	100

Mode The mode is the third measure of central tendency or typicalness. It is most relevant (in the sense of providing most useful information) for nominal or ordinal *variables*. The mode is the most frequent value or category of a *variable*. The mode in Table G.4 is "good" health. Also, as Table G.2 showed in passing within the parentheses (286 females and 184 males), the mode for biological sex is "female."

Normal distribution (Gaussian distribution)   In Figure G5, the normal distribution is superimposed on the *distribution* of the weight *variable*. The fit is not perfect. The shape of the weight *distribution* nevertheless has some resemblance with the symmetrical normal distribution. If the weight *variable* had a normal distribution, we would know (without doing any statistical analyses) that 95 percent of the students' weight in the *sample* would fall in the interval: *average* weight (72.25 kilograms) $\pm$ 2 *SDs* (13.25). The normal distribution is an important foundation for *significance testing* and the calculation of CIs.

Population   A population is a collection of all *units* having at least one common feature, such as all Norwegians allowed to vote in the national election, or all sailing boats registered in the US boat registry. While the population for the student data are all the students attending the university in question, the *sample* we study is a much smaller subset/fraction/percentage of this population.

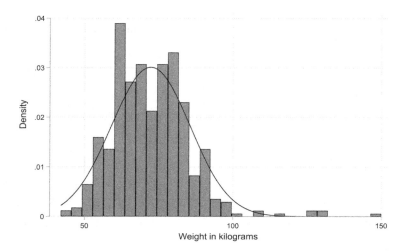

Figure G.5 Histogram of students' weight in kilograms, with perfect normal distribution superimposed

***p*-Value** A *p*-value is the outcome of a *significance test* which, in turn, evaluates whether an *association* between two *variables* is statistically significant. Statistically significant might very loosely be taken to suggest present in the population. More precisely, the *p*-value measures the probability of finding a sample association of a certain magnitude, or a larger one, given that there is no such *association* in the population. If this *p*-value is 5 percent or lower, we deem the *association* statistically significant; it is most likely present in the population.

Random sampling Random sampling implies that a random draw procedure is used to determine how some of the units in a *population* end up in a *sample*. This random mechanism is usually some lottery selection device making sure that every unit in the *population* has roughly the same and equal chance of getting into the *sample*. Random selection from the population is, to simplify, the only safe way of making sure that the resulting *sample* is representative of the *population* (akin to being a miniature model of it).

Regression and regression coefficient (regression analysis)
Regression analysis is a general extension of *correlation* analysis. Regression analysis or some version of it might "always" be used to associate two *variables*. Unlike *correlation*, regression typically boils down to summarizing the *association* between two *variables* into a straight regression line. Figure G6 adds such a regression line to the scatterplot in Figure G1.

The main thing in regression analysis is the quantification of the regression line's steepness or slope. The regression coefficient expresses this steepness. In Figure G6, this regression coefficient is 0.88. The interpretation of this regression coefficient is simple: by moving one unit (centimeter) to the right on the *x*-axis (height), the increase on the *y*-axis (weight) is 0.88 kilograms. Regression is also the solution in finding out how several *independent variables* simultaneously affect a *dependent variable*. This is called multiple regression analysis. In this regard, the multiple regression pictured in Figure G7 also includes the *variable* biological sex. The figure shows how, on average, male students are taller and weigh more than female students.

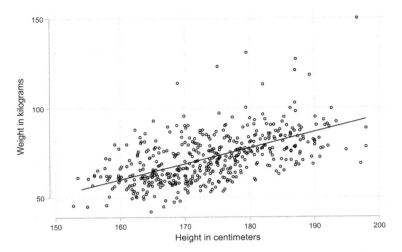

Figure G.6 Students' weight in kilograms by students' height in centimeters, with linear regression line

Note. 70 inches (or 5 feet 10 inches) is roughly 178 centimeters.

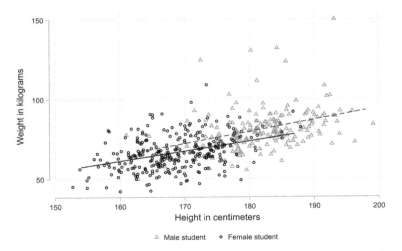

△ Male student   ○ Female student

Figure G.7 Students' weight in kilograms by students' height in centimeters and by sex, with dashed linear regression line for male students and solid regression line for female students

Note. 70 inches (or 5 feet 10 inches) is roughly 178 centimeters.

Sample   By definition, a sample is a subset or fraction of some larger *population*. In statistics, we often study samples rather than *populations* for resource reasons – be they economical, practical, or ethical. The present student sample is a random sample of the *population* of students (that is, all the students) attending a Norwegian university. If a sample is drawn by means of a *random selection* procedure, we might most often think of the sample as being representative of the larger *population* (as in being a miniature model of it).

Significance test   A significance test is used to judge whether a statistical association in a *sample* also holds up in the larger *population* from which the sample is drawn. To simplify grossly (cf. Chapters 4 and 7), we ask if random chance differences between the *sample* and the unknown *population* might have generated the *association* we find in the sample. This question boils down to judging a *p-value*. If it is unlikely that random differences between the *sample* and the *population* are somehow responsible for the sample *association* (generating a p-value of 5 percent or less), we deem the *association* "statistically significant." As such, we claim that the *association* probably exists in the *population*.

Standard deviation (SD)   The SD measures the variation around the *average* of a variable, akin to the CV. Technically, the SD is the square root of the variance. The key issue is that the larger the SD, the further away from the *average* the typical *unit* is located (or the larger the variation there is). The SD for the weight *variable* in the student data is 13.25.

Statistical association (see association)

Units (observations)   The units are the entities we have *variable* information, or *data*, on. The units are often people in the social and behavioral sciences, but they could be (almost) anything. In the student data, the units are, well, students.

Variable   A variable is anything that varies between or among *units*. The *units* in the student data are students, and the variables height and age (and so on) vary among these students in the *data*. Some students are taller (or older), some are shorter (or younger), and some students are of *average* or *median* or modal (*mode*) height or age. The same reasoning applies to weight, sex, and cardio exercise.

Variable value or category   Any *variable* may take on a set of values, as in a student being 22, 23, 24, or 25 years old and so on. When a *variable* takes on only a small number of values, like for nominal variables (e.g., day of week), ordinal variables (e.g., Likert-scale), and dummy variables (e.g., yes or no), we often use the term categories rather than values.

x-variable (see independent variable)

y-variable (see dependent variable)

REFERENCES

Aggerwal, C. C. (2017). *Outlier Analysis.* Springer International Publishing: New York.

Agresti, A. (2010). *Analysis of Ordinal Categorical Data.* Second Edition. John Wiley: Hoboken, NJ.

Agresti, A. (2018). *Statistical Methods for the Social Sciences.* Fifth Edition. Pearson Education Ltd: London.

Alexander, N. (2015). What's More General Than a Whole Population? *Emerging Themes in Epidemiology,* 12 (11), 1–5.

Allison, P. D. (1999). *Multiple Regression. A Primer.* Pine Forge Press: Thousand Oaks, CA.

Allison, P. D. (2002). *Missing Data.* Sage Publications, Inc.: Newbury Park, CA.

Anscombe, F. J. (1973). Graphs in statistical analysis. *American Statistician,* 27, 17–21.

Bailor, A. J., and Pennington, R. (2023). *Statistics Behind the Headlines.* CRC Press: Boca Raton, FL.

Békés, G., and Kézdi, G. (2021). Data Analysis. For Business, Economics, and Policy. Cambridge University Press: Cambridge.

Bergstrom, C. T, and West, J. D. (2020). *Calling Bullshit. The Art of Skepticism in a Data-Driven World.* Random House: New York.

Berk, R. A. (2004). *Regression Analysis. A Constructive Critique.* Sage Publications, Ltd: Thousand Oaks, CA.

Best, H., and Wolf, C. (2015). The Sage Handbook of Regression Analysis and Causal Inference. Sage Publications, Ltd: London.

Bueno de Mesquita, E., and Fowler, A. (2021). *Thinking Clearly with Data. A Guide to Quantitative Reasoning and Analysis.* Princeton University Press: Princeton, NJ.

Clark, T., Foster, L., Sloan, L., and Bryman, A. (2021). *Bryman's Social Research Methods.* Sixth Edition. Oxford University Press: Oxford.

Cunningham, S. (2021). *Causal Inference: The Mixtape.* Yale University Press: London.

Freedman, D., Pisani, R., and Purves, R. (2007). *Statistics*. Fourth Edition. W.W. Norton & Company: New York.

Gelman, A., Hill, J., and Vehtari, A. (2021). *Regression and Other Stories*. Cambridge University Press: Cambridge.

Gelman, A., and Vehtari, A. (2024). *Active Statistics*. Cambridge University Press: Cambridge.

Gillham, N. W. (2001). *Sir Francis Galton. From African Exploration to the Birth of Eugenics*. Oxford University Press: New York.

Gladwell, M. (2011). *Outliers. The Story of Success*. Back Bay Books: New York.

Gorard, S. (2021). *How to Make Sense of Statistics*. Sage Publications, Ltd: Thousand Oaks, CA.

Harford, T. (2020). *How to Make the World Add Up. Ten Rules for Thinking Differently About Numbers*. The Bridge Street Press: London.

Huntington-Klein, N. (2022). *The Effect. An Introduction to Research Design and Causality*. CRC Press: Boca Raton, FL.

Kennedy-Shafer, L. (2024). Teaching the Difficult Past of Statistics to Improve the Future. *Journal of Statistics and Data Science Education*, 32, 108–119.

Kline, R. B. (2020). *Becoming a Behavioral Science Researcher. A Guide to Producing Research that Matters*. Second Edition. The Guilford Press: New York.

Meuleman, B., Loosveldt, G., and Emonds, V. (2015). Regression Analysis: Assumption and Diagnostics. In Best, H., and C. Wolf (2015). *The Sage Handbook of Regression Analysis and Causal Inference*. Sage Publications, Ltd: London, 83–110.

Pearl, J., and Mackenzie, D. (2018). *The Book of Why. The New Science of Cause and Effect*. Basic Books: New York.

Reinhart, A. (2015). *Statistics Done Wrong*. No Starch Press, Inc: San Francisco, CA.

Ritchie, S. (2020). *Science Fictions. How Fraud, Bias, Negligence, and Hype Undermine the Search for Truth*. Metropolitan Books: New York.

Rosenbaum, P. R. (2017). *Observation and Experiment. An Introduction to Causal Inference*. Harvard University Press: Cambridge, MA.

Salsburg, D. (2017). *Errors, Blunders, and Lies. How to Tell the Difference*. CRC Press: Boca Raton.

Schneider, J. W. (2013). Caveats for Using Statistical Significance Tests in Research Assessments. *Journal of Informetrics*, 7, 50–62.

Spiegelhalter, D. (2019). *The Art of Statistics – Learning from Data*. Penguin Books: London.

Stanton, J. M. (2001). Galton, Pearson, and the Peas: A Brief History of Linear Regression for Statistics Instructors. *Journal of Statistics Education*, 9, 1–13.

Stigler, S. (2016). *The Seven Pillars of Statistical Wisdom*. Harvard University Press: Cambridge, MA.

Thrane, C. (2019). Expert Reviews, Peer Recommendations and Buying Red Wine: Experimental Evidence. *Journal of Wine Research*, 30, 166–177.

Thrane, C. (2020). *Applied Regression Analysis. Doing, Interpreting and Reporting.* Routledge: New York.

Thrane, C. (2022). Thrane, C. (2022). *Doing Statistical Analysis: A Student's Guide to Quantitative Research.* Routledge: New York.

Thrane, C. (2024a). Using Composite Performance Variables to Explain Football Players' Market Values. *Managing Sport and Leisure.* https://doi.org/10.1080/23750472.2024.2305902

Thrane, C. (2024b). Helt i mål. Lær statistisk tenkning med tall fra sportens verden. Humanist Forlag: Oslo, Norway.

Thrane, C., and Haugom, E. (2020). Peer Effects on Restaurant Tipping in Norway: An Experimental Approach. *Journal of Economic Behavior and Organization*, 176, 244–252.

Thrane, C., Lien, G., Mehmetoglu, M., and Størdal, S. (2024). Price Hedonics of Beers: Effects of Alcohol Content, Quality Rating, and Production Country. *Journal of Agricultural & Food Industrial Organization.* https://doi.org/10.1515/jafio-2023-0048

Wheelan, C. (2014). *Naked Statistics.* W.W. Norton & Company: New York.

INDEX

Printed in the United States
by Baker & Taylor Publisher Services